Confiscated Properties of Philipse Highland Patent Putnam County New York

1780 - 1785

Compiled by

William T. Ruddock

HERITAGE BOOKS
2012

HERITAGE BOOKS
AN IMPRINT OF HERITAGE BOOKS, INC.

Books, CDs, and more—Worldwide

For our listing of thousands of titles see our website
at
www.HeritageBooks.com

Published 2012 by
HERITAGE BOOKS, INC.
Publishing Division
100 Railroad Ave. #104
Westminster, Maryland 21157

Copyright © 2012 William T. Ruddock

Other Heritage Books by the author:

*Linen Threads and Broom Twines: An Irish and American Album and Directory
of the People of the Dunbarton Mill, Greenwich, New York, 1879–1952
Volume 1: The Album*

*Linen Threads and Broom Twines: An Irish and American Album and Directory
of the People of the Dunbarton Mill, Greenwich, New York, 1879–1952
Volume 2: The Directory*

All rights reserved. No part of this book may be reproduced or transmitted in any form or by any means, electronic or mechanical, including photocopying, recording or by any information storage and retrieval system without written permission from the author, except for the inclusion of brief quotations in a review.

International Standard Book Numbers
Paperbound: 978-0-7884-5385-4
Clothbound: 978-0-7884-3445-7

Content

Background	5
An Apology	7
Drama	7
Table of Property Transactions	8
Maps of Confiscated Property	22
Name Index	55
Place Index	61

Acknowledgements

This project was only possible because my wife Eldonna has allowed me the time and her patience while I pursue projects like this.

The Putnam County Clerk's office has been very helpful in providing me copies of the Concklin Maps.

The New York State Archives has been most helpful in providing me with their copy of confiscated property deeds.

The Church of Jesus Christ of Latter Day Saints Family History Library provided a complete copy of Volume 8 of Dutchess County Deeds

The following 7.5 Minute Quadrangle maps were provided courtesy of the US Geological Survey: Wappingers Falls, Hopewell Junction, Poughquag, Pawling, West Point, Oscawaha Lake, Lake Carmel, Brewster, Peekskill, Mohegan Lake, Croton Falls, and Peach Lake.

Background

During the Revolution, various states enacted laws that allowed for the confiscation and sale of land which was held by known loyalists. In New York, the 3rd State Legislature passed the 22 October 1779 Act of Attainder in which 59 persons were named as "Adherents to the enemies of the State." These individuals were attained and their estates, real and personal, were confiscated by the State. In addition, those on the list were " each and every of them who shall at any time here after be found in any part of the State, shall be, and are hereby adjudged and declared guilty of felony, and shall suffer Death as in cases of felony, without Benefit of Clergy." Four of those on the list were Roger Morris, Esq. late member of the Council for the Colony of New York, Mary Morris his wife, Beverly Robinson and Susannah Robinson, his wife.[1]

As heirs of their father, Frederick Philipse, Mary Morris and Susannah Robinson held life estates in approximately 2/3rds of the Philipse Highland Patent. Mary and Susannah's brother, Philip Philipse, held the other 1/3rd. During the Revolution this land was the southern part of Dutchess County. Most all of the Highland Patent property would later become part of present day Putnam County, New York. At the time of the 1779 act, there were several hundred farmers leasing land in the Highland Patent from the Robinson and Morris families. During the period of 1780 till 1785 most but not all of this land was sold to the famers who were leasing this land. Original records of these property transactions are found in two places: Volume 8 of Dutchess County Deeds and at the State Archives of New York.

The original Highland Patent was divided into 9 large lots consisting of Water lots 1 -3 were located along the Hudson River, "Long" lots 4 – 6 that extended from the northern to the southern boarder of the patent, and lot 7 – 9 on the eastern boarder of the patent.

The properties confiscated were Robinson Water Lot # 1, Morris Water Lot # 3, Robinson Long Lot # 4, Morris Long Lot # 4 , Robinson Lot # 7 and Morris Lot # 9. Starting in 1885 and ending in 1887, Henry S. Concklin drew maps out maps of the confiscated lots based on property descriptions in the Volume 8 of Dutchess County Deeds.

All of these maps except Robinson Water Lot # 1 are on file at the Putnam County Clerk's office as follows:

Morris Lot # 3 Map file #s 05-009.1 & 05-009.2
Morris Lot # 5 Map File #s 01-075(1), 01-075(2), 01-075(3), & 01-075(4)

---

[1] Thomas Jones, *History of New York during the Revolutionary War: and of the Leadin Events in the Other Colonies at that Period*, (New York: New York Historical Society, 1879), vol. 2, pp. 269-270. The complete act of Attainder may be found at pp. 510-523.

Morris Lot # 9 Map File #s 07-008(1) & 07-008(2)
Robinson Lot # 4 Map File #s 06-016(1), 06-016(2), 06-016(3), & 06-016(4)
Robinson Lot # 7 Map File #s 04-016(1) & 04-016(2)

Although, they are not the subject of this book, Concklin also drew maps of the Philipse lots 2, 6 and 8 based on later property transfers and these too are on file with the Putnam County Clerk.

Large Lots of Putnam County

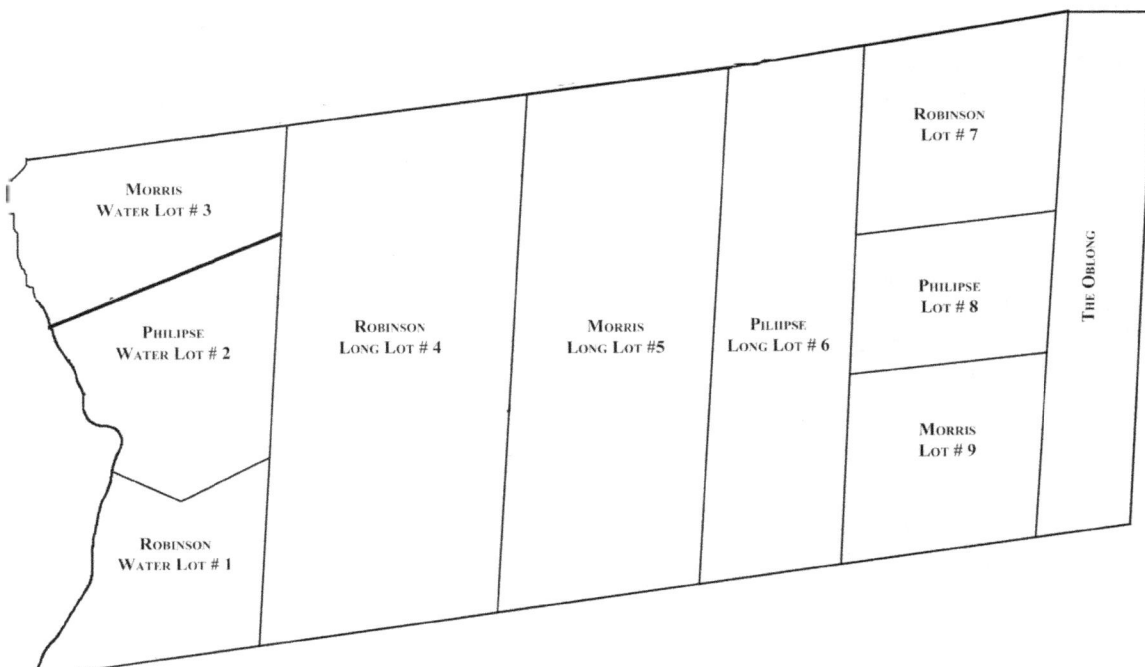

While the Concklin maps are useful they have many drawbacks:

1) They were based on the 1780s property descriptions. Much has changed in the geography of Putnam County since that time. Often it is nearly impossible based on these maps to locate a particular property.
2) They are in very poor condition. Many areas of these maps are very dark while others are very light. This makes reading the information on the maps a challenge.
3) It appears that Concklin did no begin with a good based map of area. His positions for key features are often off by 100s of feet..

The purpose of this book is to attempt, as best as possible, to recover the Concklin maps by cleaning them up and re-annotating them. They were then overlaid onto current USGS maps to form a composite map that includes both Concklin and USGS information. This allows a researcher to easily find properties relative to today's features. Because of the scale of the properties this mapping has been spread out over 32 pages.

The property descriptions themselves often contain additional information not found on the maps themselves. For this reason a table of relevant property transactions has been included before the maps in this work. This table includes information about each property transaction, including the parties involved, the date, the amount of the transaction, and based on the Volume 8 property descriptions, the farms, streams, bodies of water, and neighbors boarding on each property.

An Apology

I feel I must caution the reader. I am neither a draftsmen nor a cartographer. There are bound to be errors in these maps that I have introduced, or repeated from Concklin. So I apologize in advance. My primary interest in doing this was to help researchers (most of whom I would expect to be genealogists or historians) with their quest to understand where people lived at a point in time.

Historical Drama

There is a fair amount of drama in the story of the Highland Patent confiscation. As mentioned above, Morris and Robinson only held life estates in these lots. The remainder was to go to their children. Technically all the State of New York could seize from them were life estates. But the State of New York sold the properties as freehold. After the war both families went to England and both sold their reversionary rights to John Jacob Astor for $100,000 per family. Mr. Astor sued the State of New York and won a settlement of $500,000. I would encourage the reader to consult both Blake and Pelletreau for a the history of how the Robinson and Morris families came into these properties and full account of these interesting events in New York History.[2]

---

[2] William J. Blake, *The History of Putnam County, N.Y.: WITH AN ENUMERATION OF ITS TOWNS, VILLIAGES, RIVERS, CREEKS, LAKES, PONDS, MOUNTAINS, HILLS, AND GEOLOGICAL FEATURES; LOCAL TRADITIONS, SHORT BIOGRAPHICAL SKETCHES OF EARLY SETTLERS,* (New York:, Baker & Scribmer, 1849), p. 182-186; William Smith Pelletreau, *History of Putnam County, New York; With Biographical Sketches of Its Prominent Men,* (Philadelphia: W.W. Preston, 1886), pp. 20-64, & 87-101.

Table of Property Transactions

Table of Property Transactions

Sequence	Prior Owner	Buyer	Price	Date	Location	Farm # or Other	Boarders and Neighbors Mentioned	Current Occupier
2	Robinson	Luddington, Comfort	4000	1 Nov 1780	Fredricksburgh		Farm 32; Willis, Jedediah; Farm 31; Mooney, Robert; Mill Brook: and Saw Mill	
3	Robinson	Oakley, Elijah	2000	4 Dec 1780	Fredricksburgh		Muddy Brook; Farm 25; Bog Meadow; Farm 55; Croton River: and Farm 56	
4	Robinson	Frisby, Caleb	2000	20 Dec 1780	Fredricksburgh	??	Farm 20; Rockey Ridge; Small Brook; and Farm 27	
5	Robinson	Hill, David	1500	20 Dec 1780	Fredricksburgh	13	Farm 12; Akin, David on Farm 12; The Colony; The Oblong; Croton River: Farm 14; Menzies, Thomas on Farm 14; and Akin, Joseph on Farm 13	
6	Robinson	Crawfoot, Joseph	1200	20 Dec 1780	Fredricksburgh		Coveys, John; and Wolf, Sarah	
7	Robinson	Kidd, Alexander	3000	20 Dec 1780	Fredricksburgh	50	Croton River; Farm 49; and Farm 48	
8	Robinson	Close, David	500	20 Dec 1780	Fredricksburgh	36	Beadsley, Andrew; The Road; Mooney, Robert; and Burch, Jonathan	
9	Robinson	Hayes, James	4560	20 Dec 1780	Fredricksburgh	19 & 20	Farm 18; Farm 29; ABrook; and Farm 21	Utter, Amos
11	Robinson	Warrin, Epharim	2150	20 Dec 1780	Fredricksburgh	??	Farm 29	
12	Robinson	Newberry, John	2000	20 Dec 1780	Fredricksburgh	39	Utters; and Benjamin	
14	Robinson	Hecock, David	4100	19 Dec 1780	Fredricksburgh	54 & 55	Farm 52; and Croton River	
15	Robinson	Wilcox, Roswell	4000	20 Dec 1780	Fredricksburgh		Hecock, David; Sunken Bog Meadow; and Hecock, David	
16	Robinson	Burch, John	1200	20 Dec 1780	Fredricksburgh		Newberry, John; and Bryant, Dr. Samuel	
19	Robinson	Carley, Peter	1.15.0	28 Mar 1781	Fredricksburgh	House	Johnson, Samuel; Post, John; and Luddington, Comfort	
20	Robinson	Bennet, Increase	5.10.0	23 Apr 1781	Fredricksburgh	House	Croton River; and Shaw, Daniel	
21	Robinson	Post, Anthony	350	29 Mar 1780	Fredricksburgh		Luddington, Comfort; Johnson; and Carley, Peter	
22	Robinson	Delavan, Nathaniel	2092.1	15 Mar 1881	Fredricksburgh		Croton River; Ward, Stephen, Esq.; and Wright, Dennis	Mitchell, Thomas
23	Robinson	Frisbey, Caleb	3000	1 Apr 1781	Fredricksburgh	28 of Lot 7	Farm 27; Farm 26; Medow, Sunken Bog; and Farm 26	
24	Robinson	Stibbens, Nehemiah	17750	19 Apr 1781	Fredricksburgh		Burch, Widow; and Ferris, Reed	Burch, John
26	Robinson	Birdsall, Benjamin & Henry Luddington	250	19 Apr 1781	Fredricksburgh		Croton River; Atkins, David; The Oblong; Hill, David; and Atkins, Josiah	
27	Robinson	Mills, Samue; Bardsley, Benajah; Bowbridge	18200	19 Apr 1781	Fredricksburgh	forty ?	Croton River; Farm 50; Farm 39; Farm 40; Farm 43: and Farm 46	
28	Robinson	Delavan, Samuel	269.1	19 Apr 1781	Fredricksburgh		A Brook; Phillips, Jacob; and A Meadow	
29	Robinson	Mills, Samuel; bowbridge, Billey, Beardsley, Benajah	7500	19 Apr 1781	Fredricksburgh		Burch, John, Widow of David	Burch, Widow of David
30	Morris	Hunt, Jesse	445	20 Apr 1781	?		Mill Brook; and Ellis, Jacob	Vermillion, John, Late
31	Robinson	Wallace, Uriah	10350	20 Apr 1781	Fredricksburgh		Newberry, John	Prindle, Lettice
32	Robinson	Pell, Samuel T.	400	20 Apr 1781	Fredricksburgh	57	Muddy Brook; Crosby, Nathan; Duer, William; and Croton River	Pell, Phillip, Esq.
33	Robinson	Luddington, Comfort	1800	21 Apr 1781	Fredricksburgh		Dibbles, David; Scott, Peter; and Close, David, Rev.	
34	Robinson	Phillips, James	200	20 Apr 1781	Fredricksburgh		Patterson, Mathew, Esq.; Croton River; Lindsey, David; and Bridge, Croton	
35	Robinson	Weed, Jehial; Weed & Ambler, John	1000	23 Apr 1781	Fredricksburgh		Frisby, Caleb; Coveys, James; Utters, John; and Utters, Amos	
36	Robinson	Shaw, Daniel	70	23 Apr 1781	Fredricksburgh		Road; Patterson, Mathew; and Mill Brook	
36-a	Robinson	Smith, William	2750	see p. 11			Highway; Saw Mill; and Pond, Heustins	
37	Morris	Smith, William	110	16; 1781	Fredricksburgh		Mills, Robinson; Highway; and Saw Mill	
38	Robinson	Towner, Samuel	12025	1 Apr 1781	Fredricksburgh	61	Phillips, Phillip; Muddy Brook; Farm 46; Farm 25; Kidd, Joseph on farm 25: Farm 23; and Kidd, Joseph on Farm 25	Robinson, Beverly
39	Robinson	Wyllis, Jedediah	3350	27 Apr 1781	Fredricksburgh	32	Bog Meadow; Phillips, Jacob; Luddington, Comfort; Mooney, Robt; and Hecock, David	
41	Morris	Phillips, Ebenezer	218.14.0	30 Apr 1781	Fredricksburgh		Mill Brook; Gove, John; and The River	Warner, Jesse
42	Robinson	Mitchell, Thomas	152.10.0	30 Apr 1781	Fredricksburgh		Croton River; and Ward, Stephen, Esq.	Melgram, Alexander
43	Robinson	Hans, Asa	4000	1 May 1781	Fredricksburgh		Muddy Brook; Pell, Phillip; Croton River; Pell, Samuel; and The Road	
44	Robinson	Morris, Robert	21650	1 May 1781	Fredricksburgh		Croton River; Mitchell, Thomas; Sands, Comfort; and Birdsall, John	Akins, David
45	Robinson	Willis, Jedediah	2000	1 Apr 1781	Fredricksburgh		Lott, Four Mile	Ballard, Tracy
46	Robinson	Duer, William, Esq.	197500	2 Apr 1781	Fredricksburgh		Muddy Brook; Farm 5; and Hains, Asa	Crosby, Nathan

Table of Property Transactions

Sequence	Prior Owner	Buyer	Price	Date	Location	Farm # or Other	Boarders and Neighbors Mentioned	Current Occupier
47	Robinson	Morris, Robert	10450	10 May 1781	Fredricksburgh		Farm 41; Highland, Patent; Upper, Patent; Farm 43; and Croton River	Chase, Daniel
48	Robinson	Newberry, John	45	1 May 1781	Fredricksburgh		Luddington, Comfort; Burch, Jonathan; and Newberry, John	Newberry, John
49	Robinson	Covey, James	2200	2 May 1781	Fredricksburgh		Wolfs, Sarah; and Covey, John	
50	Robinson	Post, Anthony	20.0.0	3 May 1781	Fredricksburgh		Wall, Stone	
51	Robinson	Hecock, David	3000	20 Dec 1780	Fredricksburgh		Phillips, Jacob	
55	Robinson	Burch, John	24.0.0	1 May 1781	Fredricksburgh		Luddington, Comfort; Burch, John; and Newberry, John	
56	Robinson	Jones, Epharim	1500	2 May 1781	Fredricksburgh		Hatch, Timothy; and Phillips, Phillip	Jones, Epharim
58	Robinson	St. John, Abraham	2500	2 May 1781	Fredricksburgh		Hill, Great; Jones, Epharim; Utters, John; Utters, Amos; Robinson, John: and Ballard, Tracy	
59	Robinson	Sands, Comfort	17400	1 Apr 1781	Fredricksburgh		The Oblong; Birdsall, John; Highway; Chase, WedW; Gifford, Benjamin: Delavan, Nathaniel; Akins, David; and Duer, William, Esq.	Wright, Dennis
60	Robinson	St. John, Abraham	600	1 Apr 1781	Fredricksburgh		Towners, Samuel; Birdsall, Abraham; and Hatch, Timothy	Chandler, Joseph
61	Robinson	Sands, Comfort	9800	1 Apr 1781	Fredricksburgh		Pell, Phillip; Crosby, Nathan; Duer, William; Croton River; and Haynes, Asa	Palmer, William
62	Robinson	Smith, William	2750	16 May 1781	Fredricksburgh		Farm Mill; Graham, Charles; Clark, Abigal; Laclare, John; Highway : and Pond, Hustin	Smith, William
64	Robinson	Burch, Jonathan	5050	24 Oct 1780	Fredricksburgh	34	Farm 31; and Phillips, Phillip	Burch, Jonathan
65	Morris	Gregory, Ezra	106	4 Jan 1782	Fredricksburgh		Foster, Duke; Hains; Pierce, Isaac; and Gregory, Josiah	Gregory, Ezra
66	Morris	Brown, Jonathan	723	17 Jan 1781	Fredricksburgh		a Brook; Howes, Moody; Paddock, Seth; Cranes, Jonathan; Paddock, Silas: Richards, Moses; Richards, Ezra; Townsend; Dickenson & Bull Mill; and Road	Brown, Jonathan
67	Morris	Crane, Jonathan	265.1	2 May 1781	Fredricksburgh		Oblong; Paddock; Brown, Jonathan; and Paddock, Silas	Crabe, Jonathan
68	Morris	Mead, Edmond	139.14.0	26 Dec 1781	Fredricksburgh		Burlin; Mill River; Cedar Pond Brook; Wallace, Uriah; Townsend, Christopher: Grove; Matine; and Lockwood, Timothy	Mead, Edmond
69	Robinson	Shaw, Daniel	177.6.8	3 May 1781	Pawlings		Algers, William; Main Road; Stephens, Nathaniel; Grant, James; Croton River: Ferris, Reed; Van Wert, Isaac; and Swamp, Bog	Cain, John
70	Morris	Graham, Charles	790	1 Jun 1781	Fredricksburgh		Cocks, James; and Brook	Angevine, WedW
71	Morris	Drake, John	262	1 Jun 1781	Fredricksburgh		Gregory, Joseph; Mabey; and Townsend, Benjamin	Drake, John
72	Morris	Hyatt, Abraham	135	1 Jun 1781	Fredricksburgh		Dutch South Line; Bog Meadow; Highway; Beardslee; and Trowbridge	Whitney, Jeremiah
73	Morris	Gregory, Joseph	83	1 Jun 1781	Fredricksburgh		Highway; Drake, John; Mills, Samuel; and Dutch South Line	Gegory, Joseph
74	Morris	Crane, John	82	1 Jun 1781	Fredricksburgh		Berry, Jabez; and Highway	Crane, John
75	Morris	Berry, John	12.13.9	1 Jun 1781	Fredricksburgh		Highway; and Lott, Phillip	Berry, John
77	Robinson	Calkins, James	29	1 Aug 1781	Fredricksburgh		Oblong; Sands, Comfort; Wright, Daniel; and Chase, Widow	Calkins, James
81	Morris	Leek, Phillip	232.4.0	20 Aug 1781	Fredricksburgh		Bloomer, William; Gage, Moses; and Pond	
83	Morris	Howes, Moody	192	1 Oct 1781	Fredricksburgh		Croton River; and Dickerson, John	Howes, Moody
84	Morris	Sacket, James	207	1 Oct 1781	Fredricksburgh	14	Farm 7; Croton River; and Lott, Mill # 8	Townsend, Robert
85	Morris	Townsend, Isaac	149.12	1 Oct 1781	Fredricksburgh		Farm 26	Townsend, Isaac
86	Morris	Paddock, Seth	264	1 Oct 1781	Fredricksburgh		Howes, Moody; Brown, Jonathan; Road; Oblong; and Croton River	Paddock, Seth
87	Morris	Green, Nathan	124.1	1 Oct 1781	Fredricksburgh	29	Croton River; Farm 27; and Farm 28	Green, Nathan
88	Morris	Lowrie, Thomas	90	1 Oct 1781	Fredricksburgh		James, John; and Croton River	Delavan, Abraham
89	Morris	Paddock, Silas	144	1 Oct 1781	Fredricksburgh		Monument, Road; and Oblong	Paddock, Silas
90	Morris	Gove, John	547.11.0	1 Oct 1781	Fredricksburgh		Mill Brook; and Mead, Edmond	Ward, Isreal
91	Morris	Delavan, Timothy	95.8.0	1 Oct 1781	Fredricksburgh		Dan, John; and Westchester, Line	Delavan, Timothy
92	Morris	Crosby, Benjamin & Enoch	383	1 Oct 1781	Fredricksburgh		Ellis, Jacob; Townsend, Uriah; and Creek, The	Hains, Samuel
93	Morris	Crosby, Benjamin & Enoch	144.4.0	1 Oct 1781	Fredricksburgh		Croton River; and Waring, Thaddeus	Bailey, Jeremiah
94	Morris	Field, Stephen	428	10 Nov 1781	Fredricksburgh	18	Farm 16; and Farm 16	Field, Stephen

Table of Property Transactions

Sequence	Prior Owner	Buyer	Price	Date	Location	Farm # or Other	Boarders and Neighbors Mentioned	Current Occupier
95	Morris	Horton, Joshua	200	10 Nov 1781	Fredricksburgh	46 in Lot 5	Farm 47; Dutton, William; and Austin, Jonathan	Rodes, John
96	Morris	Bouton, Jehial	91.12.6	10 Nov 1781	Fredricksburgh		Road; Westchester, Line; Palmer, Caleb; and Nickerson, Wedow	Bouton, Jehial
97	Robinson	Boyd, Ebenezer	134.8	10 Nov 1781	Fredricksburgh		Odle, Benjamin; Wiltsey, Daniel; and Oakley, William	Concklin, Stephen
98	Morris	Smith, Mourice	180	10 Nov 1781	Fredricksburgh		Charlick, Henry; Winter, Moses; Carpenter, Ephraim; Grist Mill; and A Brook	Moss, Joseph
99	Morris	Smith, Mourice	70	10 Nov 1781	Phillips		Post Road; Husted, Joseph; Division, The; and Phillips, Phillip	Odle, Jonathan
100	Robinson	Drake, Samuel	20.8.0	10 Nov 1781	Phillips		Drake, John (son of William); and Owen, Jonathan	Drake, Samuel
101	Robinson	Drake, Samuel	74.15	10 Nov 1781	Phillips		Creek; Dutch South Line; and Owen, Jessey	Drake, Peter
102	Robinson	Paine, Joseph	64.7	10 Nov 1781	Phillips		Creek, By Bridge; and Boyds, Ebenezer	Odle, Benjamin
103	Robinson	Rosekrans, James	500	10 Nov 1781	Fredricksburgh		Meeting House; Patterson, Esq.; Kidd, Esq.; Post, Anthony; Phillips: and Church, Episcopal	Delavan, Samuel
104	Morris	Delavan, Nathaniel	330.12.0	10 Nov 1781	Fredricksburgh		Westchester, Line; and Croton River	Gomans, John & Jonathan
105	Robinson	Mooney, Robert	73	24 Dec 1781	Fredricksburgh		St. Johns; Waring; Road; and Phillips, Phillip	??
106	Morris	Richards, Ezra	168.6.0	26 Dec 1781	Fredricksburgh		None Mentioned	Richards, Ezra
107	Morris	Crosby, Solomon	108	27 Dec 1781	Fredricksburgh		Waring, Thaddeus; Green, Nathan; Highway; and Waring, Thaddeus	Crosby, Solomon
108	Morris	Ellis, Jacob	146	28 Dec 1781	Fredricksburgh		Mill River	Ellis, Jacob
109	Morris	Bailey, Peleg	76.18.6	28 Dec 1781	Fredricksburgh		Croton River; Crosby, Benjamin; Road; Green, Nathan; Nott, Nathaniel: Wallace, Uriah; and Townsend, Christopher	Bailey, Peleg
110	Morris	Pinckney, Frederick	22	28 Dec 1781	Fredricksburgh		Highway	Pinckney, Frederick
111	Morris	Loveless, William	43	28 Dec 1781	Fredricksburgh		Road; Lott, Four Mile; and Roberts, Peter	Loveless, William
112	Morris	Richards, Moses	155.14.0	3 Jan 1782	Fredricksburgh	19	Farm 7; Farm 11; Farm 18; and Farm 16	Richards, Moses
113	Morris	Hains, Mary	270.18.0	3 Jan 1782	Fredricksburgh		Wood, Nehemiah; Foster, Duke; Phillips; Wainer, Jesse ; Gregory, Ezra: Scribner, Nathaniel; Townsend, Uriah; and Mill River	Hains, Widow Mary
114	Morris	Pearce, Isaac	113.0.0	4 Jan 1782	Fredricksburgh	48	Farm 46; and The West Line	Pearce, Isaac
115	Morris	Platt, John	88.4.0	4 Jan 1782	Fredricksburgh	19	Farm 18	Platt, John
116	Morris	Rice, Edward	215	4 Jan 1782	Fredricksburgh		Paddock, David; Oblong; Dickenson; Road; Cowen, David: Pinkney; North Line of Morris Lot Line; Oblong; Lewis, Ichabod; and Monument, Oblong	Rice, Edward
117	Morris	Paddock, David, Jr.	197	4 Jan 1782	Fredricksburgh		Rice, Edward; Line Oblong; Dickerson; and Croton River	Paddock, David, Jr.
118	Morris	Nickerson, Hannah	229	5 Jan 1782	Fredricksburgh	24	Farm 23; Croton River; Farm 18; and Farm 22	Nickerson, Hannah
119	Morris	Wood, Nehemiah	229	5 Jan 1782	Fredricksburgh		Doty, Abner; Croton River; Townsend, John; Grove, John; Matine, John: Warner, Jesse ; Hains, John; and Foster, Duke	Wood, Nehemiah
120	Morris	Field, John	354	7 Jan 1782	Fredricksburgh		Paddock, Silas; The Oblong; Field, Joseph; Pond; Pelton, Phillip: Leak, Phillip; Gage, Moses; Platts, John; Richards, Moses; and Monument, Road	Field, John
121	Morris	Wallace, Uriah	69	7 Jan 1782	Fredricksburgh		Bailey, Peleg; Nott, Nathaniel; Townsend, Christopher; Townsend, John; and Mead	Bailey, Samuel
122	Morris	Mead, Jeremiah	111	8 Jan 1782	Fredricksburgh	15	Farm 14; and Croton River	Mead, Jeremiah
123	Morris	Cowen, David	92	8 Jan 1782	Fredricksburgh		Pinkney, Frederick; Rice, Edward; Townsend; Crosby, Solomon; and Dickerson, John	Cowen, David
124	Morris	Townsend, John	100	8 Jan 1782	Fredricksburgh		Doty, Abner; Mountain; Townsend, Christopher; Wallace, Uriah; Mead , Edmond: Grove; and Wood, Nehemiah	Townsend, John
125	Morris	Dan, John	192	9 Jan 1782	Fredricksburgh		Delavan, Timothy; Platts, John; Westchester, Line; Field, Solomon; and Field, Stephen	Dan, John
126	Morris	Paddock, Zachariah	153	9 Jan 1782	Fredricksburgh		Cowen, David; Crosby, Solomon; and Townsend, Daniel	Paddock, Zachariah

Table of Property Transactions

Sequence	Prior Owner	Buyer	Price	Date	Location	Farm # or Other	Boarders and Neighbors Mentioned	Current Occupier
127	Morris	Gage, Moses	197	9 Jan 1782	Fredricksburgh		Delavan, Timothy; Bloomer, William; Leak, Phillip; The Road; and Platts	Gage, Moses
128	Morris	Dickerson & Bull, John & Daniel	17	9 Jan 1782	Fredricksburgh		Brown, Jonathan; Sacket, James; Crosby, Benjamin; and Brook	Dickerson & Bull, John & Daniel
129	Morris	Dickerson, John	210	9 Jan 1782	Fredricksburgh		Crosby, Solomon; Cowen, David; Rice, Edward; Paddock, David; Green, Nathan; Howes, Moody; Croton River; and Waring, Thaddeus	Dickerson, John
130	Morris	Cock, James	6	10 Jan 1782	Fredricksburgh		Hustins Island; and Pond, Hueston	
132	Robinson	Post, Anthony; Patterson, Mathew; Kidd, Alexander	195	1 Mar 1782	Fredricksburgh		Birch, John; Mills, Samuel; Stibbens; Gore, The; Gilchrist, William: and Luddington, Comfort	Post, Antony
139	Morris	King, Herman	184	29 Mar 1782	Fredricksburgh		Farm 96; Haskin, Joseph; Burling, Ebenezer S.; Brown, Josiah; and Phillips, South Line	King, Herman
140	Morris	Slutt, Michael	167	29 Mary 1782	Fredricksburgh		The Brook; Pond, Cranberry; Farm 29; The East Line; and Farm 57	Slutt, Michael
141	Morris	Folkner, Josiah	143	30 Mar 1782	Fredricksburgh	42 of Lott 5	Farm 11; The West Line; and Farm 43	Folkner, Josiah
142	Morris	Avory, John	159	30 Mar 1782	Fredricksburgh		Highway; Roads, Isaac; McLean, John; Berry, John; Smith, John: Bryon, Thomas; and ,	Avory, John
144	Morris	Bedeau, Peter	217	19 Apr 1782	Fredricksburgh		Brook; Pond, Heady; Farm 13; Farm 15; Farm 6: and Brook	Bedeau, Peter
145	Morris	Berry, Jabez	188	19 Apr 1782	Fredricksburgh		Dam Mill; Farm 58; Farm 53; Farm 60; and Pond, Long	Berry, Jabez
146	Morris	Mabee, Peter	188	19 Apr 1782	Fredricksburgh		, saite(?); Farm 55; Farm 28; Farm 30; Pond, The Great: Farm 26; The East Line; Farm 27; and Farm 29	Maybee, Peter
148	Morris	Wixsom, Peleg & Shubal	193	19 Apr 1782	Fredricksburgh		Farm 52; Farm 51; Farm 53; Pond; Farm 59: and Pond, Long	Wixsom, Peleg & Shubal
149	Morris	Pinckney, Isreal	114	19 Apr 1782	Fredricksburgh		Craft, Chimney of John's House; and Hitchcock, William	Pinckney Isreal
150	Morris	Chadwick, Comfort	68	19 Apr 1782	Fredricksburgh		Road , ; Mills, William Smith's; and Lockwood, Ebenezer	Chadwick, Comfort
151	Morris	Smith, Col. William	172	20 Apr 1782	Fredricksburgh	15 of Lott 5	Small Brook; Still Water River; Farm 7; Farm 16; Farm 17: Farm 14; Farm 36; Farm 34; Farm 37; and Hill, Captain	
152	Morris	Haight, John	256	20 Apr 1782	Phillips		Post Road; North Line; Mountain; A Brook; Hill, The: and Wright, William	
153	Morris	Wright, William	125	20 Apr 1782	Phillips		Philips Line; Rock, Split; Weeks, Gilbert; Haight, Captain; and Post Road	
154	Morris	Doty, Abner	90	20 Apr 1781	Fredricksburgh		Croton River; Wood, Nehemiah; Townsend, John; and Townsend, Christopher	Doty, Abner
155	Morris	Cock, James	131	20 Apr 1781	Fredricksburgh		Small Brook; Knaps, Moses; and Vorkaneer, Josiah	How , John
156	Morris	Hitchcock, William	178	20 Apr 1781	Fredricksburgh		Pinkney, Isreal; and Lockwood, Ebenezer	Hitchcock, William
157	Morris	Banker, Peter	149	20 Apr 1781	Fredricksburgh		Pond, Heady; Farm 6; Farm 4; West Line; and Farm 9	Banker, Peter
158	Morris	Jean, John	194	20 Apr 1781	Fredricksburgh		Croton River; Delavan, Abraham; , ; Field, Stephen; Richards, Ezra: and Mead, Jeremiah	Jean, John
159	Morris	Field, Solomon	267	20 Apr 1781	Fredricksburgh		Dan, John; Westchester Line; Platts, John; Field, Stephen; and Palmer, Caleb	Field, Solomon
160	Morris	Palmer, Caleb	75	20 Apr 1782	Fredricksburgh		Field, Solomon; Westchester Line; Field, Stephen; Nickerson; and Bouton, Jehinel	Palmer, Caleb
161	Morris	Crane, Lewis, Carpenter, John. Sarah, Caleb	360	22 Apr 1782	Fredricksburgh		Farm 62; Farm 63; Pond, The Long; and East Line	Carpenter, Wd Hannah
162	Morris	Surrine, Charles	198	22 Apr 1782	Fredricksburgh		Clark, Abigal; Gregory, Joseph; and Graham, Charles	Surroin, Charles
163	Morris	Gregory, Joseph	130	22 Apr 1782	Fredricksburgh		Pond, ; Clark, Abigal; Surrine, Charles; and Drake, Capt. John	Gregory, Joseph
164	Morris	Merrit, John	94	22 Apr 1782	Fredricksburgh		West Line; Cock , James; and Badde, Isaac	
165	Morris	Yeomans, William	122	22 Apr 1782	Fredricksburgh		a sall Brook; Farm 14; Farm 15; Farm 36; Farm 38: and Farm 12	Yeomans, William

Table of Property Transactions

Sequence	Prior Owner	Buyer	Price	Date	Location	Farm # or Other	Boarders and Neighbors Mentioned	Current Occupier
167	Morris	Crab, John	143	22 Apr 1782	Fredricksburgh		Hill, Capt. William; , ; Pinkney, Isreal; and Rock, Large	Crab, John
168a	Morris	Smith, William	71	23 Apr 1782	Fredricksburgh		Road; Farm Mill; Pond, Mill; and Dam, Mill	Hill, Wid.
169b	Morris	Smith, William	314	30 May 1782	Fredricksburgh		Pond, Kich; Dam; LeClere, John; Brook; and Hustin, Robert	Smith, William
169c	Morris	Smith, William	71	30 May 1782	Fredricksburgh		Wixson, Peleg; Crab, John; Rock, Large; Hill, Capt.; Agar, Charles: and Stokom, Jonathan	Smith, William
169d	Morris	Smith, William	314	30 May 1782	Fredricksburgh		Pond, Kich; Dam; LeClere, John; Brook; and Hustin, Robert	Kich, Thomas
169e	Morris	Smith, William	71	30 May 1782	Fredricksburgh		Wixson, Peleg; Crab, John; Rock, Large; Hill, Capt.; Agar, Charles: and Stokom, Jonathan	Kich, Thomas
170	Morris	Surrione, James	111	31 May 1782	Fredricksburgh		Brook; Pond, Heady; Farm 8; Farm 5; and Farm 7	Surroin, James
171	Morris	Le Clare, John	89	31 May 1782	Fredricksburgh		Great, Pond; Farm 51; and Farm 16	Le Clare, John
172	Morris	Wisenfells, Charles F.	137	31 May 1782	Fredricksburgh		Small Brook; Knaps, Moses; Nelson, Mahar; Haight, Samuel; and Cook, Jas.	Elsworth, John
173	Robinson	Oakley, Robert	221	1 Jun 1782	Phillips		Brook; Road; and Brook	Oakley, Robert
174	Morris	Berry, John	141	1 Jun 1782	Fredricksburgh		Brook; Pond; Roads, Isaac; Avory, John; and Smith, John	Bea, Isaac
174	Morris	McLean, John	141	1 Jun 1782	Fredricksburgh		Brook; Pond; Roads, Isaac; Avory, John; and Smith, John	Bea, Isaac
175	Morris	Oakley, John	111	1 Jun 1782	Fredricksburgh		Slut, Michael; Adams, John; Berry, John; and Bolden, James	Oakley, John
176	Morris	Gearnau, John	72	3 Jun 1782	Fredricksburgh		Pond; Maybee, Peter; Brook; Pond, Cranberry; and Slut, Michael	Gearnau, John
178	Morris	Smith, David	318	3 Jun 1782	Fredricksburgh		Farm 61; Farm 63; Farm 71; Croton River; and East Line	Smith, David
179	Morris	Nott, Nathaniel	98	3 Jun 1782	Fredricksburgh		Grun, Nathan; Bayley, Peleg; Wallace, Uriah; Pond, Cedar Pond; Cedar Pond Brook: Mead ; Haskin, Joseph; and Loveless, William	Nott, Nathaniel
180	Morris	Hoskin, Joseph	174	3 Jun 1782	Fredricksburgh		Roberts, Peter; Loveless, William; Nott, Nathaniel; Burling; and King, Heman	Haskin, Joseph
181	Morris	Wood, Robert	24	5 May 1781	Fredricksburgh		N/A	Willet, Gilbert
182	Morris	Cole, Ebenezer	36.5	3 Jun 1782	Fredricksburgh		Barret, Isaac; Brook; Croton River; Hopkins, Solomon; and Russell, Robert	
183	Dickinson	Pelton, Philip & Daniel & Benjamin	59	4 Jun 1782	Fredricksburgh		Ellis, James; Lott, 6; Beaver Brook; Bridge, ; and Green, Benjamin	Pelton, Daniel & Philip & Benjamine
184	Morris	Russegue, Isaac	130	4 Jun 1782	Fredricksburgh		Road; Foster, Duke; Perces, Isaac; Ganung, John; Yeoman, : and Croton River	Russegue, Isaac
185	Morris	Ganung, John	170	4 June 1782	Fredricksburgh		Farm 49; Croton River; The West Line; and Courtland Manor, Line	Ganung, John
186	Morris	Haigt, Gilbert	48	6 June 1782	Fredricksburgh		Haigt, Samuel; Arway, Charles; and Anderson, Peter	Haigt, Gilbert
187	Morris	Lounsbury, Isaac	202	6 June 1782	Fredricksburgh		Fam, 17; Still Water River; Brook; and Farm 21	Lounsbury, Isaac
188	Robinson	Lockwood, Gilbert	137	6 June 1782	Phillips		N/A	Read, Isaac
189	Morris	Field, William	100	7 Jun 1782	Fredricksburgh		Creek, The	Field, William, Townsend, Uriah
190	Morris	Trobridge, Billy; Bardsley, Benajah	287	7 Jun 1782	Fredricksburgh		Westchester, Line; Highway ; Gregory, Joseph; Graham, Charles; Lounsbury, Isaac: and Hoyat, Abraham	Trobridge, Billy
191	Morris	Stokom, Jonathan	97	7 Jun 1782	Fredricksburgh		Pond, Kirk; Hill, Wedow; Rock, Large; and Brook	Stokom, Jonathan
192	Robinson	Owen, Jesse	188	7 Jun 1782	Phillips		Acker Kill; Farm 19; Courtland Manor, Acker; Farm 22; Peeks Kill: Farm 21; and Fam, 16	Owen, Jesse
193	Morris	Agar, Charles	84	7 Jun 1782	Fredricksburgh		Stokom, Jonathan; Highway ; Smith, William; and Brooks, Two	Agar, Charles
194	Robinson	Platt, Zephaniah; Bailey, John, Jr.	495	10 Jun 1782	Phillips		Robinson, Long Lott; Peekskill Road; Roads, Shanadore; Smith, Elijah; The East Line: Pettit Meadow; Clift, High; Moras; and Yeoman, Samuel	Taylor, Isaac

Table of Property Transactions

Sequence	Prior Owner	Buyer	Price	Date	Location	Farm # or Other	Boarders and Neighbors Mentioned	Current Occupier
197	Robinson	Swartwout, Jacobus	469	10 Jun 1782	Phillips		Griffin, Jacob; and Taylor, Thomas	Purdy, Wedow
198	Robinson	Griffin, Jacob	397	10 Jun 1782	Phillips		Rombout & Phillips Line; and Corner, Northwest of Lott	Crawford, William
199	Robinson	Swartwout, Jacobus	110	10 Jun 1782	Phillips		Griffin, Jacob	Purdy, Wedow
200	Robinson	Christian, Richard, Jr.	152	11 Jun 1782	Phillips		Pond,	Christian, Richard, Jr.
201	Robinson	McDonald, John	112	11 Jun 1782	Phillips		McKabe, Mathew; and Mountain, Top	McDonald, John
202	Morris	Bryant, Thomas	129	11 Jun 1782	Fredricksburgh		Roads, Isaac; Farm 26; Farm 13; Farm 4; Farm 25: Farm 6; and Farm 5	Bryan, Thomas
203	Morris	Roads, Isaac	221	11 Jun 1782	Fredricksburgh		Avory, John; Highway; Bryant, Thomas; Covert, Sylvenus; Lane, Nathan : and Bogg Meadow	Roads, Isaac
204	Robinson	Lane, George	239	11 Jun 1782	Phillips	9	Farm 10; Farm 11; Farm 12; Farm 8; Brook: Farm 2; Farm 1; and Courtland Manor,	Lane, George
205	Morris	Brower, Hannah	98.5	11 Jun 1782	Fredricksburgh		Courtland Manor, Line; Smith, Joseph; Hoyat, John; O'Byan, Catherine; Knap, Daniel: and Courtland Manor, Line	Horton, Joseph
206	Morris	Cole, Elijah, Jr.	117.5	11 Jun 1782	Fredricksburgh		Pond, Long; Carver, Timothy; Adams, Thomas; Cole, Joseph; and Cole, Daniel	Cole, Elijah, Jr.
207	Morris	Cole, Elijah	396	11 Jun 1782	Fredricksburgh		Croton River; Farm 62; Farm 61; Farm 63; Farm 70: Adams, Thomas; Pond, ; Dam, ; Barret, Isaac; and Croton River	Cole, Elijah
208	Morris	Barrett, Isaac	121	13 Jun 1782	Fredricksburgh		Cole, Elijah; Pond Mill; and Brook	Barrett, Isaac
209	Robinson	Dusenbury, William	305	15 Jun 1782	Phillips		Brook; and Gager, Nathaniel	Dusenbury, William
210	Morris	DelavanSamuel, William	112	15 Jun 1782	Fredricksburgh		Arwas, Charles; Brook; Anderson, Peter; Lockwood, Ebenezer; Hitchcock, William: and Haight, Gilbert	Austin, Jonathan
214	Robinson	Barager, John	213	7 Oct 1782	Phillips		Dusenbury, Moses	Barager, Peter
215	Robinson	Perry, James	150	17 Oct 1782	Phillips		Pond, Large; Christian, Richard, and Field, Anthony	Perry, James
216	Morris	Austin, Isaac	92	17 Oct 1782	Fredricksburgh		Highway; Mahar, Nelson; Knap, Moses; Newman, William; Hill, William: and Anderson, Peter	Austin, Isaac
223	Morris & Robinson	Lane, Nathan	278	4 Nov 1782	Fredricksburgh		Brook; Hyatt, John; dividing two precints Line; O'Byan, Catherine; Arway, Charles: Banker, Peter; Roads, Isaac; Covert, Sylvenus; and Knap, Hannah	Lane, Nathan
224	Morris & Robinson	Smith, John	95	4 Nov 1782	Fredricksburgh		Folkner, Josiah; Smith, Solomon; McLean, John; Berry, John; Brook: Folkner, Josiah; and Smith, Solomon	Smith, John
225	Morris & Robinson	Kirkham, Thomas & Zebedee	336	12 Nov 1782	Fredricksburgh		Farm 1; Farm 2; Farm 5; Still Water Brook; and Courtland Manor, Line	Kirkham, Zebedee & Thomas
226	Morris	Heroy, Charles	112	12 Nov 1782	Fredricksburgh		Still Water River; Farm 3; Farm 2; Farm 6; and Brook	Heroy, Charles
227	Morris	Adams, John	90.75	13 Nov 1782	Fredricksburgh		Slut, Michael; Oakley, John; Berry, John; Highway; and Crane, John	Adams, John
228	Morris	Dunn, James	30.75	13 Nov 1782	Fredricksburgh		Russell, Robert; Pond, Minthorn; and Barret, Isaac	Dunn, James
229	Morris	Vanscoy, Abel	120	13 Nov 1782	Fredricksburgh		Pond, Minthorn; Russell, Robert; and Door, Mary Chase	Vanscoy, Abel
230	Morris	Hughson, Robert	163	13 Nov 1782	Fredricksburgh		Pond, The Large; Crane, John; Garnaus, John; Road; Wicksom, Peleg; and Pond, the small	Hughson, Robert
231	Morris	Knap, Daniel	162.5	14 Nov 1782	Fredricksburgh		Courtland Manor, Line; Brower, Hannah; O'Byan, Catherine; and Kirkum, Thomas & Zebulon	Knap, Daniel
232	Morris	Russel, Robert	162.25	14 Nov 1782	Fredricksburgh		Pond, Minthorn; Dun, James; Barret, Isaac; and Vanscoy, Abel	Russel, Robert
233	Robinson	Hyatt, John, Nathaniel, & Joshua	457	14 Nov 1782	Phillips		Peekskill Highway; Fishkill Highway; Bridge, ; Lott, 2; , West LIne of tract: Beaver Dam Brook; Christian, Richard; and Satterly, Richard	Hyatt, John, Nathaniel, Joshua
234	Robinson	Hyatt, John, Nathaniel, & Joshua	457	14 Nov 1782	Phillips		Corner, East of Lott 1; Lott, 3; West LIne of tract Line; and Lott, 1	Hyatt, John, Nathaniel, Joshua

Table of Property Transactions

Sequence	Prior Owner	Buyer	Price	Date	Location	Farm # or Other	Boarders and Neighbors Mentioned	Current Occupier
235	Robinson	Hyatt, John, Nathaniel, & Joshua	457	14 Nov 1782	Phillips		Corner, East of Lott 2; Roads, two meet; Montross, Peter; Wynn, John; Gray, John: and Lott, 2	Hyatt, John, Nathaniel, Joshua
236	Morris	Secor, John	124.75	14 Nov 1782	Fredricksburgh		Pond, Heady; Secor, Isaac; Baddeau, Isaac; Baddeau, Peter; and Brook	Secor, John
237	Morris	Secor, Isaac	124	14 Nov 1782	Fredricksburgh		To Heady Brook; Knap, Moses; Yeoman, William; Merritt, John; and Pond, Heady	Secor, Isaac
238	Morris	Vanscoy, Jacob	88	14 Nov 1782	Fredricksburgh		Russel, Robert; Highway; Russel, Thomas; Hopkins, Solomon; and Cole, Ebenezer	Vanscoy, Jacob
239	Morris	Davis, John	116	14 Nov 1782	Fredricksburgh		Corner, Brook & Highway; Fuller, Robert; Vansqoit, Jacob; Russel, Thomas; Hopkins, Isaiah: and Brook & Highway Brook	Davis, John
240	Morris	Knap, Moses	230	15 Nov 1782	Fredricksburgh	Lott 12 of Lott 5	Feeds Heady Brook; Farm 44; Farm 43; Farm 41; Farm 38: and Farm 13	Knap, Moses
241	Morris	Carver, Timothy	350	16 Nov 1782	Fredricksburgh		Pond, Long; Farm 63; Farm 70; Farm 50; Farm 52: and Farm 60	Carver, Timothy
242	Morris	Clark, Abigail	132	16 Nov 1782	Fredricksburgh		Pond; Farm 31; Farm 17; Farm 16; Brook: Pond, Great; and Farm 33	Clark, Abigail
243	Robinson	Smith, Solomon	163	18 Nov 1782	Phillips		East of Lott 4 Line; Farm 5; Farm 7; Farm 29; Farm 25: and Farm 27	Smith, Solomon
244	Morris	Lockwood, Ebenezer	144	18 Nov 1782	Fredricksburgh		Hitchcock, William; and Chadwick, Comfort	Lockwood, Ebenezer
245	Morris	Bedeau, Isaac	94.5	18 Nov 1782	Fredricksburgh		Bedeau, Peter; Secor, John; Merrit, John; and Cock, James	Bedeau, Isaac
246	Morris	Beya, John	132	18 Nov 1782	Fredricksburgh	farm 19 of lott 5	Farm 18; Hill Water River; Farm 20; Courtland Manor, Line; Farm 3: and Still Water River	Beya, John
247	Robinson	Knap, Hannah	222	18 Nov 1782	Phillips		Lane, Nathan; Covert, Sylvenus; Pond, ; Brook; Concklin, Mary: Lane, George; and Hyatt, John	Knap, Hannah
248	Morris	Pelton, Philip; Myrich, Joshua	43	18 Nov 1782	Phillips		Highway; Avory, John; Banker, Peter, Dec; McLean; Berry: and Rhodes, Isaac	Curry, George
249	Robinson	Post, Abraham	252	18 Nov 1782	Phillips	Farm 29 of Lott 4	Farm, 20; Farm, 30; Farm, 7; Farm, 6; and Farm, 28	Post, Abraham
250	Robinson	Armstrong, John	280	18 Nov 1782	Phillips	Farm 52 of Lott 4	Small Brook; Farm, 49; Farm, 50; and Farm, 51	Armstrong, John
251	Morris	Sylvenus, Covert	49	19 Nov 1782	Fredricksburgh		Lane, Nathan; Pond, The; Leading to Pond Brook; and Rhodes, Isaac	Covert, Sylvenus
252	Morris	Haight, Gilbert	60.75	19 Nov 1782	Fredricksburgh		Spring; Mahar, Nelson; Haight, Samuel or Gilbert; Heady, William; Haight, Home Place: and Anderson, Peter	Haight, Samuel
253	Morris	Mahar, Nielson	132.5	19 Nov 1782	Fredricksburgh		Highway; Knap, Moses; Austin, Isaac; Anderson, Peter; and Weisenfell, Charles F.	Mahar, Nelson
254	Robinson	Dusenbury, Moses	115.25	19 Nov 1782	Phillips		Brook; Creek, ; and Dusenbury, William	Dusenbury, Moses
255	Morris	Higby, William	128	19 Nov 1782	Fredricksburgh		Courtland Manor, Line; Gregory, Joseph; and Hughson, Jeremiah	Higby, William
256	Robinson	Drake, John	271	19 Nov 1782	Phillips	Farm 24 lott 4	Peeks Kill; Sherwood, Joseph; Farm, 23; and Lanes Brook	Drake, John
257	Robinson	Owens, Jesse	82	19 Nov 1782	Phillips	Farm 21 lott 4	Peeks Kill; Farm, 16; and Farm, 20	Wiltsey, Henry
258	Morris	Hopkins, Isaiah	83	19 Nov 1782	Fredricksburgh		Brook; Davis, John; and Pond,	Hopkins, Jesse
259	Robinson	Dusenbury, Moses	217.25	20 Nov 1782	Phillips		Creek, ; Wiltsey, Daniel; Dusenbury, William; and Brook	Dusenbury, Moses
260	Robinson	Penier, Isaac	55	20 Nov 1782	Phillips	Farm 1 of Lott 4	Courtland Manor, Line; Lott, Roger Morris's Long; Road; and Farm, 2	Smith, Joseph
261	Robinson	Concklin, Mary	270	20 Nov 1782	Phillips	Farm 11 of Lott 4	a small Brook; Farm, 10; Farm 17; Farm 12; Farm 13: Farm 26; Pond, Knaps; Farm 8; Farm 9; and another small Brook	Concklin, Mary
262	Morris	Charlick, Henry	383	21 Nov 1782	Fredricksburgh		Smith, Morris; Winter, Moses; Morris, Mary; Nickerson, Edward; Rondle, Joseph: and Kill	Charlick, Henry

Table of Property Transactions

Sequence	Prior Owner	Buyer	Price	Date	Location	Farm # or Other	Boarders and Neighbors Mentioned	Current Occupier
263	Robinson	Denny, John	106.75	20 Nov 1782	Phillips		Pond, ; Concklin, Mary; Tompkin, Nathaniel; O'Bryant, Thomas ; Rhodes, Isaac: and Brook	Denny, John
264	Robinson	Tompkins, Cornelius	240	20 Nov 1782	Phillips	Farm 14 of Lott 4	Farm 13; Farm 25; and Farm 27	Tompkins, Cornelius
265	Robinson	Higby, Daniel	220	20 Nov 1782	Phillips	Farm 25 of Lott 4	Farm 14; Farm 28; Farm 6; and Farm 27	Higby, Daniel
266	Robinson	Field, Anthony	500	20 Nov 1782	Phillips	Farm 50 of Lott 4	Farm 49; Farm 64; Pond, Long; and Farm 52	Field, Anthony
267	Robinson	Denny, Richard	80.5	21 Nov 1782	Phillips		Water Line; and Lotts, Water	Denny, Richard
268	Morris	Miller, Jonathan	106.5	21 Nov 1782	Phillips		Highway; White, William; Field, Anthony; McCabe, Mathew; McDonald, John: Bugby, Daniel; and Tompkins, Cornelius	Miller, Jonathan
269	Robinson	Cromwell, Samuel	239	21 Nov 1782	Phillips	Farm 10 of Lott 4	From Knaps pond Brook; Pond, Knapps; Farm 9; Courtlands Manor, Line; Farm 17: a small Brook; and Farm 11	Cromwell, Samuel
270	Robinson	Travis, Titus	116	21 Nov 1782	Phillips		Farm 6; Bugby, Daniel; Miller, Jonathan; and McDonald, John	Travis, Titus
271	Robinson	Frost, Jedediah	143	21 Nov 1782	Phillips		Kannopus Road	Frost, Jedediah
272	Robinson	Archer, Gabriel	172	21 Nov 1782	Fredricksburgh	Farm 36 of Lott 4	Lanes Brook; Farm 33; Farm 37; and Farm 41	Archer, Gabriel
273	Robinson	Steenbach, Philip	122	21 Nov 1782	Fredricksburgh		Spring,	Steenbach, Philip
274	Morris	Adriance, Cornelius	122	20 Apr 1782	Phillips		Brook; and Haight, Capt. John	
275	Morris	Marvin, Ichabod	74	13 Jun 1783	Fredricksburgh		Crosby, Solomon; Green, Nathan; Croton River; and Dickerson, John	Marvin, Ichabad
277	Morris	Bloomer, Benjamin	460	16 Jan 1783	Phillips		Weeks, Gilbert; and Husted, Wedow	Bloomer, Benjamin
278	Morris	Adams, Thomas	270.5	16 Jan 1783	Fredricksburgh		Cole, Elijah; Cole, Elijah, Jr.; Chadwick, Comfort; Lockwood, Ebenezer ; Hitchcock, William: Carver, Timothy; and Cole, Elijah	Adams, Thomas
279	Townsend	Crane, Joseph, Jr.	75	16 Jan 1783	South East Precinct	Part of Lott 6	Connecticut Line; and Townsend, Robert, Dec	Townsend, Elihu
279	Morris	Harrington, Joseph	141	18 Nov 1783	Fredricksburgh		Charlick, Henry; Smith, Maurice; Moss, Mary; Price, ??; Haight, Amy: and Charlick, Henry	Winter, Moses
280	Morris	Bloomer, Gilbert	298	16 Jan 1783	Phillips		Hill, Break neck; Hudson River; mouth Brook; and Philips & Morris Line	Bloomer, Gilbert
281	Robinson	Rickey, Peter	287	16 Jan 1783	Phillips		Canopus River; Owen, Jonathan; and Cudney, Jeremiah	Rickey, Peter
282	Morris	Hughson, Jeremiah	315	16 Jan 1783	Fredricksburgh		Courtlandts Manor, Line; Higby, William; Mabee, Abraham; Drake, John; and Gregory, Joseph	Hughson, Jeremiah
283	Morris	Russel, Thomas	166	16 Jan 1783	Fredricksburgh		Russel, Robert; Vanscoy, Jacob; and Davis, John	Russel, Thomas
284	Robinson	Hill, Thomas	370	16 Jan 1783	Phillips		Brook; Bard, Joseph; Canopus Road; Frost, Jedediah; and by a brook Highway	Hill, Thomas
285	Morris	Hustis, Joseph	296	17 Jan 1783	Phillips		Brook; Post Road; at Post Road Brook; and Husted, Wedow	Hustis, Joseph
285	Morris	Barton, John	180	17 Jan 1783	Phillips		Smith, Morris; and a to Husted's farm Brook	Barton, John
286	Morris	Barton, John	180	17 Jan 1783	Phillips		Husted, Joseph	Barton, John
288	Morris	Hustis, Wedow Charity	219	24 Jan 1783	Phillips		Weeks, Gilbert; Meadow; and Post Road	Hustis, Wedow Charity
289	Robinson	Christian, Richard, Sr.	331	24 Jan 1783	Phillips		Brook; and Armstrong, John	Christian, Richard
289	Morris	Dubois, Peter	293	24 Jan 1783	Phillips		Rombout & Philips Line; Hudson River; Cromwell, Wedow; and Ter Boss, Daniel	Dubois, Peter
290	Morris	Dubois, Peter	293	29 Jan 1783	Phillips		,	Dubois, Peter
292	Robinson	Crawford, William	281	27 March 1783	Phillips		Griffen, Jacob	,
293	Robinson	Gilchrist, William	97	28 Mar 1783	Pawlings		Chandler, Joseph; Turner, Nathan; Warden, Nathaniel; Newman, Nathaniel; and Patterson & Co. Line	Dibbla, David
295	Robinson	Fairley, James	119	3 Apr 1783	Fredricksburgh	Part of subdivision called lot number 7	Oblong Line; Hunt, Thomas; Lot [farm]), 1; , ; Gifford, Oblong: and Lot [farm], 2	Haviland, Isaac
296	Robinson	Fairley, James	229	3 Apr 1783	Fredricksburgh	Part of subdivision called lot number 7 is farm 5 on map of Jonathan Hampton	Farm 7; Farm 8; Oblong Line; and Farm 3	Chase, Widow

Table of Property Transactions

Sequence	Prior Owner	Buyer	Price	Date	Location	Farm # or Other	Boarders and Neighbors Mentioned	Current Occupier
297	Morris	Knap, Isreal	120	4 Apr 1783	Fredricksburgh		East West Line; Rombout Line; Carie, Samuel; Knap, Benjamin; and Shanadore Road	Knap, Isreal
313	Morris	Farington, Joseph	310	8 Apr 1783	Fredricksburgh		Leading to Fishkill Highway; and Boyds, Ebenezer	,
314	Morris	Hopkins, Solomon	341	10 Apr 1783	Fredricksburgh		West Branch Croton River; Cole, Elisha; Smith, Davis; Morris & Philips Line; and Brook	Hopkins, Solomon
315	Robinson	Tompkins, Reuben	217.5	11 Apr 1783	Phillips		N/A	
316	Robinson	Delavan, Daniel	370	11 Apr 1783	Phillips		Meek, John; and Owen, Jonathan	
317	Robinson	Vantassel, WidW. Hester	123	11 Apr 1783	Phillips		Farm 37; Farm 40; Farm 42; and Farm 36	
318	Robinson	Hunt, Thomas	25	11 Apr 1783	Pawlings		Oblong Line	
319	Robinson	Hunt, Thomas	264	11 Apr 1783	Pawlings		in west of Oblong Road; Oblong Line; Terry, Peter; along Jonathan Akins Road; Akins, Jonathan: Bond, Moses; Grant, James; and Tompkins, Jonathan G.	
322	Robinson	Odle, Oliver	172	12 Apr 1783	Phillips		Christian, Richard; Tompkins, Reuben; Brook; McDonald, John; McKabe, Mathew: and Armstrong, John	Odle, Oliver
323	Robinson	McCable, Mathew	193	12 Apr 1783	Phillips		Field, Anthony; Miller, Jonathan; Armstrong, John; Odle, Oliver; and McDonald, John	
324	Morris	Knap, Benjamin	127.5	14 Arp 1783	Fredricksburgh		Knap, Isreal; Carle, Samuel; Horton, Thomas; Knap, Isreal; Knap, Isreal: and Knap, Isreal	Knap, Benjamin
326	Morris	Hitchcock, William	36	14 Apr 1783	Fredricksburgh		Longwell, David; and Arway, Charles	
328	Robinson	Willsie, Daniel	130	7 Jun 1782 (?)	Phillips	Farm 16	Farm 15; Farm 35; Peeks Kill; Farm 20; Farm 18: and Farm 17	Willsie, Daniel
329	Robinson	Chandler, Joseph	131	2 Jun 1783	Pawlings		Farm 36; Philip Philips Line; and Farm 35	Chandler, Joseph
330	Morris	Vanamber, John	346.75	2 Jun 1783	Phillips		Hudson River; Brook; to West Point Road; Burch, Daniel; and another Brook	Vanamber, John
331	Morris	Gee, Ezekiel	200	2 Jun 1783	Phillips		N/a	
332	Morris	Townsend, Christopher	122	2 Jun 1783	Fredricksburgh		Croton River; Bailey, Peleg; Wallace, Uriah; Meed, Edmond; Townsend, John: and Doty, Abner	Townsend, Christopher
333	Robinson	Drake, Samuel	500	2 Jun 1783	Phillips		Hyatt, John & Co.; Drake, Joshua; Corner, Westerly of this tract; and Pelton, Philip	Grey
334	Robinson	Drake, Joshua	500	2 Jun 1783	Phillips		Drake, Samuel; Hyatt, John & Co.; and Jacocks, James	
335	Robinson	Hopkins, Solomon	250	2 Jun 1783	Phillips		Philips & Fredrickburg Line; and Hyatt, John & Co.	Shaw, William
336	Morris	Hopkins, Solomon	220	2 Jun 1783	Fredricksburgh		Fredricksburgh & Phillips Line; Russel, John; Hunt, Elijah; and Krankright, Teunis	Williams, Francis
337	Morris	Hopkins, Solomon	28	7 Jul 1783	Fredricksburgh		Pond, Coles; Chadwick, Comfort; Frost, David; Hughson, Jeremiah; Kniffin, Jacob: Courtlandts Manor, Line; Hustin; and Mabey, John	
338	Robinson	Horton, John	140	2 Jun 1783	Phillips		Pond, Long; Hyatt, John & Co.; Odle; Post; Bell, Peter: and Colegrove, William	Formerly Yeoman, Anthony
339	Robinson	Jacocks, James	162	2 Jun 1783	Phillips		Drake, Samuel's Large farm; and Highway	Gee, Ezekiel
340	Morris	Wiltsie, Martin	59	7 Jun 1783	Phillips		Bloomer, Gilbert; Hudson River; Phillips & Morris Line; Hudson River; Hudson River: and Marsh, Capt. Dubois	At North end, Bloomer
341	Robinson	Owens, Jonathan	272.25	13 Jun 1783	Phillips		Westchester & Dutchess Line; Water Lott, Robinson's; Drake, Samuel; The Brook; and Delavan, Daniel	Owens, Jonathan
342	Robinson	Owens, Jonathan	312	13 Jun 1783	Phillips		Bashford, Thomas; Lockwood, Gilbert; The Brook; Smith, Thomas; Read, Jacob; Highway; and Likely, John	Owens, Jonathan
343	Morris	Howkins, Samuel	54	14 Jun 1783	Fredricksburgh		The Brook; Townsend, James; Ballard, William; Morris & Philips Line; Taylor, Daniel: Sprague, Jeremiah; and The Brook	Hawkins, Samuel
344	Morris	Ballard, William	93.75	14 Jun 1783	Fredricksburgh		Pond, Pine; Morris & Philips Line; Hawkins, Samuel; Townsend, James; Light, Henry: and Hopkins, Isaiah	Ballard, William

Table of Property Transactions

Sequence	Prior Owner	Buyer	Price	Date	Location	Farm # or Other	Boarders and Neighbors Mentioned	Current Occupier
345	Robinson	Odle, Amos	46.5	14 Jun 1783	Phillips		Odle, Oliver	Odle, Amos
346	Robinson	Post & Odle, Henry & Isaac	227.5	14 Jun 1783	Phillips		Van Tassel, Easter; Steenbauck, Philip ; and Bard, Joseph	
347	Robinson	Smith & Read, Thomas & Jacob	134.5	14 Jun 1783	Phillips		Lanes Brook; Owen, Jonathan; Lockwood, Gilbert; Krankright, Sibert; Archer, Gabriel: and Highway	
348	Robinson	Bard, Joseph	184	14 Jun 1783	Phillips		Brook; Hill, Thomas; and Post, Henry	Bard , Joseph
349	Morris	Drew, Isaac	187	16 Jun 1783	Fredricksburgh		Hill, a high; Chadwick, Comfort; Hunt, Samuel ; Barret, Isaac; and Barret, James	Drew, Isaac
350	Robinson	Oakley, William	125	17 Jun 1783	Phillips		Westchester & Dutchess Line; Concklin, John; Concklin, Mary; Corner, an Old; and Dolittle	Oakley, William
351	Robinson	Hyatt & Lane, John & George	464	17 Jun 1783	Fredricksburgh		Drake, Samuel ; Steneback, Philip ; Horton, John; Pond, Long; Christian, Richard, Jr.: and Pond, a small	Hyatt, John & Company
352	Robinson	Lane, Hyatt	203	17 Jun 1783	Phillips		Hyatt, Col. John; Lane, George; Hyatt, John & Co.; Christian, Richard, Jr.; and Armstrong, John	
353	Morris	Chadwick, Comfort	117.5	17 Jun 1783	Fredricksburgh		Drew, Isaac; Hill, The top; and Meadow	Chadwick, Comfort
354	Robinson	Denny, Richard	129.5	17 Jun 1783	Phillips		East of Water Lotts Line; Jacocks, James; Brook; Gee, Ezekiel; and Denny, Richard	,
355	Morris	Obrian, John	210	18 Jun 1783	Fredricksburgh		Farm 1; Farm 4; Farm 5; and Farm 3	Obrian, Catherine
356	Morris	Boyd, Ebenezer	71	18 Jun 1783	Fredricksburgh		Jones, Samuel ; Frost, David; Pond, ; Vanscoy, Abel; Chase, Widow's old house: Highway; Chase, Widow's old house; Vanscoy, Abel; Kronkrite, Lawrence; and Carles, William	
357	Robinson	Hyatt & Penier, John & Isaac	461	18 Jun 1783	Phillips		Hyatt, John; Penier, Isaac; Hopkins, Solomon; Northwest of whole tract Line; and Pelton, Philip	
358	Robinson	Hyatt & Penier, John & Isaac	480.5	18 Jun 1783	Phillips		Platts, Zephaniah & Co.; Fredricksburgh & Phillips Line; and Northwest of whole tract Line	
359	Morris	Boyd, Ebenezer	157.5	20 Jun 1783	Fredricksburgh		Jones, Samuel ; Highway; Boyd , Ebenezer ; Wood, Mary; and Corner, Then old	Roads, Isaac
360	Morris	Frost, David	168	20 Jun 1783	Fredricksburgh		Jones, Samuel ; Chadwick; Pond, Coals; Pond, little; and Boyd , Ebenezer	Berritt, James
361	Morris	Cromwell, Judith	153	20 Jun 1783	Phillips		Hudson River; Wiltsey, Martin; Dubois, Peter; Ter Bush, Daniel; Brook: and , John	Cromwell, Judith
362	Morris	Weeks, Gilbert	285	20 Jun 1783	Phillips		Creek, Clove; Husted, Joseph; Husted, Charity; Bloomer, Benjamin; Wright, William: and Knapp, Israel	Weeks, Gilbert
364	Morris	Knap, Isreal	168	15 Oct 1783	Phillips		Barton, John; Healey, Eleazer; Hannion, David; Haight, John; Wright, William: Creek, Clove; and Weeks, Gilbert	Knap, Isreal
365	Morris	Williams, Richard	109	22 Oct 1783	Fredricksburgh		Boothe, John; and Crankite, Teunis	Williams, Richard
366	Morris	Randle, Joseph	221	22 Oct 1783	Fredricksburgh		Brook; Gharlick, Henry; Rubbleyee, Andrew; and Kill	,
367	Morris	Boothe, John	118	23 Oct 1783	Fredricksburgh		Carl , Camuel ? Samuel; Platts, Zephaniah & Co.; and Williams, Richard	Boothe, John
368	Morris	Carle , Samuel	370	23 Oct 1783	Fredricksburgh		Brook	Carrell, Samuel
369	Robinson	Budd, John	200	24 Oct 1783	Phillips		Creek; Hanion, David; Springer, Isaac; Lewis, Thomas; : and Langdon, James	,
370	Morris	Crankite, Teunis	101	25 Oct 1783	Fredricksburgh		Munger, Lemuel; and Williams, Richard	Crankite, Teunis
371	Morris	Horton, Thomas	160	25 Oct 1783	Fredricksburgh		Rumbout Line	,
373	Robinson	Langdon, James	82	18 Nov 1783	Phillips		Budd, John; and Lewis, Thomas	
374	Robinson	Baker, Squire	82.75	18 Nov 1783	Phillips		Brinkerhoof, John; Mountain, The; and Healey, Ebenezer	
375	Morris	Hanion, David	200	18 Nov 1783	Phillips		Brook; Budd, John; and Adriance	
376	Morris	Sparling, Paul	54	18 Nov 1783	Phillips		Bloomer, Benjamin; Post Road; Husted, Joseph; Meadow; and Husted, Wedow	Sparling, Paul

Table of Property Transactions

Sequence	Prior Owner	Buyer	Price	Date	Location	Farm # or Other	Boarders and Neighbors Mentioned	Current Occupier
377	Morris	Maybee, Abraham	187	18 Nov 1783	Fredricksburgh	Farm 27 in lott 5	Farm 20; Farm 24; Farm 30; Farm 29; and Farm 28	Maybee, Abraham
378	Robinson	Tompkins, Joshua	112	18 Nov 1783	Phillips		Post, Abraham; Odle, Amos; and Fredericksburgh & Phillips Line	
380	Robinson	Patterson, Mathew	250	26 Dec 1781	Fredricksburgh		Chandler, Joseph; Highway; Creek, Muddy; Oakley; and Watt, Robert	Tidd (kidd?), Joseph
381	Robinson	Alger, Wm B.	70	no date??	Fredricksburgh		Covy, James; Haycock; Robinson; and Waring, Epharim	
382	Robinson	Patterson, Mathew	157	26 Dec 1781	Fredricksburgh		Croton River	Patterson, Mathew, Esq.
389	Robinson	Gager, Nathaniel	87	17 Oct 1783	Phillips		Dusenbury, William; Tompkins, Nathaniel; and Concklin, Mary	Gager, Nathaniel
390	Robinson	Travis, Titus	118	18 Oct 1783	Phillips		Tompkins, Reuben; and Rooring Brook	
391	Robinson	Berret, Isaac	22.5	18 Oct 1783	Fredricksburgh		Fredericksburgh & Phillips Line	Simkins, John
392	Robinson	Russel, John	101	18 Oct 1783	Phillips		Fredericksburgh & Phillips Line; Hopkins, Solomon; Brook; and Travis, Titus	
393	Robinson	Ingorsel, ?	30	21 Oct 1783	Phillips		Falkiner, Josiah; Smith, John; Tompkins, Josiah; and Heady, William	
394	Robinson	Christian, John	110	22 Oct 1783	Phillips		Brook; Bard, Joseph; Hill, ; Highway; and Hill, Thomas	Brower, Teunis
395	Morris	Cushman, Consider	180	22 Oct 1783	Fredricksburgh		Hawkins, Isabell; Charlick, Henry; and Townsend, James	Cushman, Consider
396	Robinson	White, William	179	23 Oct 1783	Phillips		Tompkins, Cornelius; Highway; Miller, Jonathan; Field, Anthony; and Tompkins, Nathaniel	,
397	Morris	Hawkins, Samuel	27	23 Oct 1783	Fredricksburgh		Phillips & Morris Line; Hawkins, Samuel ; Porter, David; and Sprage, Jeremiah	Taylor, Daniel
398	Morris	Ayres, Richard	200	23 Oct 1783	Fredricksburgh		Boyd , Ebenezer ; and Monger, Lemuel	
399	Robinson	Pelton & Myrick, Philip & Joshua	500	23 Oct 1783	Phillips	Lott 1	Mountain, East of Canopus Hollow; Hyatt, John & Co.; West line of whole tract Line; and Drake, Samuel	Wynn, John
400	Morris	Berrit, Justice	130	23 Oct 1783	Fredricksburgh		Nickerson, Edward; and Townsend, Levy	Barrett, Justis
401	Robinson	Pelton & Myrick, Philip & Joshua	500	23 Oct 1783	Phillips	Lott 2	Lott, 1; and West line of whole tract Line	Wynn, John
402	Robinson	Pelton & Myrick, Philip & Joshua	178	23 Oct 1783	Phillips	Lott 3	Lott, 2; Platts, Zephaniah & Co.; and Shanadore Road	Wynn, John
403	Morris	Shaw, Robert	190	23 Oct 1783	Fredricksburgh		Chadwick, Comfort	Shaw, Robert
404	Morris	Monger, Lemuel	211	23 Oct 1783	Fredricksburgh		Ayres, Richard ; Crankright, Teunis; and Boyd , Ebenezer	Monger, Lemuel
405	Morris	Ogdon, Joseph	34	24 Oct 1783	Fredricksburgh		Corner, North East; Gore Line; Main Road; Haight, Amy; and Goodfellow, William	Ogdon, Joseph
406	Morris	Russel, John	39	24 Oct 1784	Fredricksburgh		Fredericksburgh & Phillips Line; Carles, Isaac; Brook; Travis, Titus; and Barrit, Isaac	Simkins, Robert
407	Robinson	Oakley, Gilbert	130	24 Oct 1783	Phillips		Wycope Road; Hyatt, Col. John & Co.; Bridge, ; Oakley, Wedow; Brook; and Swamp,	Oakley, Gilbert
408	Morris	Hunt, Samuel	117.5	24 Oct 1783	Fredricksburgh		Roads, John; Pelton, Philip & Brothers in Company; Hichcock, William; Barret, Isaac; and Drew, Isaac	Hunt, Samuel
409	Morris	Bell, Peter	136.5	24 Oct 1783	Phillips		lains [lanes] Brook; Colegrove, William; Horton, John; Post, Henry; Oddle, Isaac: and Archer, Gabriel	Bell, Peter
410	Morris	Vanscoy, Abel	76	24 Oct 1783	Fredricksburgh		Goodfellow, William; and Pond, White	Price, Mary
411	Robinson	Denny, Richard	114.75	24 Oct 1783	Phillips		Highway; Hill, Thomas; and Christian, John	Brower, John
412	Robinson	Tompkins, Nathan	219	25 Oct 1783	Phillips		Tompkins, Cornelius; Denny, John; Concklin, Mary; Gager, Nathaniel; and White, William	
413	Morris	Jones, Samuel	194	25 Oct 1783	Fredricksburgh		Frost, David; Chadwick, Comfort; Shaw, Robert; and Boyd , Ebenezer	Jones, Samuel
414	Robinson	Hyatt & Penier, John & Isaac	232	25 Oct 1783	Phillips		Oakley, Mary; Hopkins, Solomon; Oakley, Gilbert; and Hyatt, John & Co.	,
415	Morris	Townsend, James	352	25 Oct 1783	Fredricksburgh		Light, Henry; Davis, John ; Smalley, John ; Hawkins, Isabell; and Cushman, Consider	Townsend, James
416	Morris	Headon, William	138.5	25 Oct 1783	Fredricksburgh		Horton, Joshua; Roads, John ; and The Precinct Line	Headon, William
417	Robinson	Saterly, Richard	120.5	25 Oct 1783	Phillips		Wycopee Road; Hyatt, John & Co.; Brook; Christian, Richard ; Tompkins, Reuben: and Oakley, Gilbert	

Table of Property Transactions

Sequence	Prior Owner	Buyer	Price	Date	Location	Farm # or Other	Boarders and Neighbors Mentioned	Current Occupier
418	Robinson	Likely, John	96.75	27 Oct 1783	Phillips		Mountain, The; Owens, Joshua; Smith, Thomas; Roads, Jacob; and Van Tassel, Ester	Likely, John
420	Robinson	Ryall, Peter & John	292	29 Oct 1783	Phillips		Horton, Thomas; Rumbout & Philips Line; Smith, Elijah; Knap, Benjamin; Platts, Zephaniah & Co.: Taylor; Yeoman; Tree, The Shingle; and Falls, Buttermilk	
424	Morris	Sprage, Jeremiah	98	30 Oct 1783	Fredricksburgh		Hawkins, Samuel; Pelton & Myrick, Phillip & Joshua; and Porter, David	Sprage, Jeremiah
427	Robinson	Birdsall, Benjamin	30	5 Nov 1783	Fredricksburgh		Birdsall, Benjamin; Croton River; Hill, David; and Road	Akin, Josias
428	Robinson	Healey, Eleazer	200	18 Nov 1783	Phillips		Hannion, David; Knap, Isreal; and Healye, John	Healey, Eleazer
429	Robinson	Healey, John	208	18 Nov 1783	Phillips		Road; and Healey, Eleazer	Healey, John
430	Morris	Porter, David	190	18 Nov 1783	Fredricksburgh		Taylor, Daniel; Nickerson, Edward; Road; Dakin, Johnson; and Morris & Philips Line	Bugby, Ezekiel
431	Robinson	Colegrove, William	187	18 Nov 1783	Phillips		Pond, The Long; Bell, Peter; Lain's Brook; Kronkhight, Sibert; White, William: and Field, Anthony	
432	Morris	Haight, Amy	66	18 Nov 1783	Fredricksburgh		Carpenter, Ephraim; Brook; Highway; and Ogden	Haight, Amy
433	Robinson	Kiers, Henry	147	18 Nov 1783	Phillips		N/A	Kiers, Henry
434	Robinson	Brinkerhoff, John	244	18 Nov 1783	Phillips		Dam, Old Saw Mill; Baker, Squire; Hannion, David; Budd, John; Lewis, Thomas: pond or meadow Line; pond or meadow Line; and Lewis, Thomas	Springer, Isaac
443	Morris	Goodfellow, William	66	25 Oct 1783	Fredricksburgh		Gore Line; East West Line; Ogden, Joseph; Winter; Price, Ebenezer: and Mory, David	Goodfellow, William
444	Robinson	Sherwood, James	160	13 Nov 1783	Phillips		Lanes Brook; Lockwood, Gilbert; Barager, Peter; Wiltsey, Daniel; and Drake, John	
445	Morris	Boyd, Ebenezer	461	24 Mar 1784	Fredricksburgh		Shanadore Road; Farrington, Joseph; Lott, 2; Carles, Samuel; Fredricksburgh & Phillips Line: Hopkins, Solomon ONe of the plots of land; Barret, Isaac; Hunt, Isaac; Shaw, Robert; and The Brook	Monger, Lemuel, Less lands of John Booth, Richard Williams, and Elijah Hunt
446	Morris	Boyd, Ebenezer	110.5	24 Mar 1784	Fredricksburgh	Rebeckah	Pond, ; Smith, Seth; Price, James; Nickerson, Edward; and Porter, David	Nealy, Rebeckah
447	Morris	Boyd, Ebenezer	220	24 Mar 1784	Fredricksburgh	Number [farm?] 2	Brook; Lott, 3; Farrington, Joseph; Randle, Joseph; Lott, 1: and Carle, Samuel	
448	Morris	Boyd, Ebenezer	500	24 Mar 1784	Fredricksburgh		Randal, Joseph; Charlick, Henry; Smith, Morris ; Swamp, Large Ash; Haight, Amy: Ogdon, Joseph; Rumbout Line; and Knap, Isreal	Lee, Caleb
449	Morris	Kniffin, Jacob	260	2 Apr 1784	Fredricksburgh	Farm 26 in Lott 5	Courtlandts Manor, Line; Farm 24; and Farm 27	Kniffin, Jacob
450	Morris	Bloomer, Gilbert	187	2 Apr 1784	Phillips		Wiltsey, Martin; and Pond, a large	
451	Morris	Newcomb, Zackeus	165	7 Apr 1784	Fredricksburgh		Ryall, Peter & John; Knapp, Benjamin; Carle, Samuel; Boothe, John; and Phillips Precinct Line	
452	Morris	Wiltsey, Martin	360	20 Nov 1784	Phillips		Hudson River; Van Amburgh, John; Brook; Bush, Daniel; another Brook: and Bloomer, Gilbert	
453	Robinson	Springer, Isaac	50	4 May 1784	Phillips		House, Dwelling; Grist Mill; Lewis, Thomas; Pond; Brinkerhoff, John: Swamp; and Pine, Jonathan	
454	Morris	Rhodes, Isaac	32.75	6 May 1784	Fredricksburgh		Horton, Joshua	
455	Robinson	Pine, Jonathan	240	14 May 1784	Phillips		Springer, Isaac; Springer's Grist Mill; Lewis, Thomas; and Swartwout, Jacobus	
456	Morris	Smalley, James	232	31 May 1784	Fredricksburgh		Vanscoy, Able; Hopkins, Solomon; Townsend, James; Russel, Thomas; The Road: and Russel, Robert	
457	Robinson	Lewis, Thomas	207	2 Jul 1784	Phillips		Swartwout, Jacobus; Pond; Brinkerhoff, John; Meadow; Budd, John: and Rumbout Line	Lewis, Thomas

Table of Property Transactions

Sequence	Prior Owner	Buyer	Price	Date	Location	Farm # or Other	Boarders and Neighbors Mentioned	Current Occupier
458	Morris	Charlick, Henry	171	2 Jul 1784	Fredricksburgh		Vanscoy, Able; Winter, Moses; Nickerson, Edward; and Nealy, Rebecka	
459	Robinson	Yeomans, John	134	2 Jul 1784	Phillips		Rumbout Line; Ryal, Peter & John; Falls, Buttermilk; and Platts, & Company	Yeomans, John
460	Robinson	Christian, John	259	15 Oct 1784	Phillips		Hyatt & Lane, John & George in Company; Steenback, Phillip ; Post, Henry; Odle, Isaac; Bard, Joseph: Christian, John's other lands; and Drake, Samuel	
461	Morris	Mead, Moses	256	20 Oct 1784	Fredricksburgh		Townsend, Charles ; and Townsend, Levy	
462	Robinson	Snouck, John	280	20 Oct 1784	Phillips		Springer, Isaac; and Robinson's Long Lott & Morris's Water Lott Line	
463	Morris	Nelson, Justus	8	20 Oct 1784	Phillips		Marsh; Constitution Island; ditch; Snouck, Mathew; Hustis, Charity: and	
464	Morris	Snouck, Mathew	16.5	20 Oct 1784	Phillips		Marsh; Constitution Island; Nelson, Justus; and	
465	Robinson	Meeks, John	425	25 Oct 1784	Phillips		Cudney, Jeremiah; and Cambell, John	
466	Morris	Wiltsey, Martin	19	20 Nov 1784	Phillips		Marsh; Constitution Island; Morris & Philips Line; and Creek	
467	Morris	Farrington, Joseph	160	10 Feb 1785	Fredricksburgh		Charlick, Henry; Light, Henry; and Barrel, Justice	Townsend, Levi
468	Morris	Hawkins, Samuel	100	10 Feb 1785	Fredricksburgh		Townsend, Levy; Hopkins, Isiah Ballard, Wilm.; Townsend, James; and Meed	Light, Henry
469	Morris	Fuller, Robert	96	10 Feb 1785	Fredricksburgh		in middle Brook; in middle Highway; Davis, John ; , Jacob; Hopkins, Solomon: Townsend, Charles; Morris & Philips Line; and Pond	
470	Robinson	Bashford, Thomas	158	10 Feb 1785	Phillips	Farm 34 in Lott 4	Lanes Brook; Farm 24; Farm 32; Farm 34; Small Brook: Farm 46; and Farm 47	
471	Morris	Anderson, Nathaniel	266	10 Feb 1785	Phillips		Post Road; Sparling, Paul; and Smith, Morris	
472	Robinson	Dusenbury, Moses, Jr.	105	10 Feb 1785	Phillips		Dusenbury, Moses Other Lands; Cronk , Sibert; Mountain, The; and Dusenbury, William	
473	Robinson	Gauger, Nathaniel	123	10 Feb 1785	Phillips		Lott, Mountain Wood; Dusenbury, Moses, Jr.; Cronk , Sibert; Tompkins, Nathaniel; and Dusenbury, William	
474	Robinson	Cronk, Sibert	240	10 Feb 1785	Phillips		Dusenbury, Moses, Jr.; Gager, Nathaniel; Brook; Rhead, Jacob; and Barager, Peter	
475	Morris	Cornell, Solomon	8	10 Feb 1784	Phillips		Marsh; Constitution Island; Morris & Philips Line; Huestis, Wedow Charity; Wiltsey, Martin: and Snouck, Mathew	
476	Morris	Huestis, Charity	4	10 Feb 1785	Phillips		Marsh; Constitution Island; Creek, ; Morris & Philips Line; Cornell, Solomon: and Nelson, Justus	
477	Merritt, Joseph	Boyd, Ebenezer	194	10 Feb 1785	Fredricksburgh	Farm 76 Lott 5	N/A	Boyd, Ebenezer
478	Robinson	Tompkins, Joshua	185	10 Feb 1785	Phillips		Brook; Tompkins, Reuben; Fredericksburgh & Phillips Line; and Odle, Oliver	
479	Robinson	Tompkins, Joshua	111	10 Feb 1785	Phillips		Oakley, Gilbert; Brook; Tompkins, Reuben; Wycopee Road; and Odle, Oliver	
480	Morris	Hunt, Daniel	95	10 Feb 1785	Fredricksburgh		Horton, Joshua; Hunt, Samuel; Drew, Isaac; Shaw, Robert; Brook: Barret, Isaac; and Hopkins, Solomon	
481	Morris	Post, John	81.75	30 Jun 1785	Fredricksburgh		Rhodes, Isaac; Heady, William; Fredericksburgh & Phillips Line; and Tompkins, Joshua	
482	Morris	Ter Boss, Daniel	500	10 Feb 1785	Phillips		Dubois, Peter; Brook; Van Amburgh, John ; and Monument	
483	Morris	Ter Boss, Daniel	200	10 Feb 1785	Phillips		Bloomer, Gilbert; Bloomer, Benjamin; Weeks, Gilbert; Wright, William; and Ter Boss, Other Lands	
484	Morris	Ter Boss, Daniel	497	10 Feb 1785	Phillips		Dubois, Peter; Old East West Line; Ter Boss, other land; Ter Boss, still other; and Wright, William	
485	Morris	Bloomer, Benjamin	430	30 Jun 1785	Phillips		Post Road; Sparling, Paul; Boomer, Benjamin other lands; Morris & Philips Water lotts Line; and Smith, Mauris	Anderson, Nathaniel

Table of Property Transactions

Sequence	Prior Owner	Buyer	Price	Date	Location	Farm # or Other	Boarders and Neighbors Mentioned	Current Occupier
486	Morrison, Malcom	Pelton, Daniel & Benjamin	20	2 May 1785	Fredricksburgh		Mill River; Creek, Bever; Lott, Long; and Fowler, Caleb	Excluting farm of William Merritt
487	Robinson	Campbell, John	439	30 Jun 1785	Phillips		Westchester & Dutchess Line; Creek, Caopus; parsonage; Meek, John ; and Tract, East Bounds	
488	Morris	Van Scoy, Timothy	190	30 Jun 1785	Fredricksburgh		Barret, Justus; Mead, Moses; Porter, David; Boyd, Ebenezer ; Van Scoy, Abel: and Charlick, Henry	Nickerson, Edward
489	Morris	Deakins, Johnson	230	30 Jun 1785	Fredricksburgh		on line Road; Morris Lott 5 & Philips Lott 6 Line; Canfield, Jedediah; Pond, White; Mountain: and Porter, David	Deakins, Johnson
490	Robinson	Baker, AbrM	430	13 Jul 1785	Phillips		Frost, Jedediah; Hill, David; Bard, Joseph; Van Tassel, WedW Hester; Likely, John : Rickey, Peter; and Water Lott of Robinson Line	Baker, Abraham
491	Robinson	Budd, Gilbert	85	16 Aug 1785	Phillips	On Lott 4	Gee, Ezekiel; and Brook	
492	Robinson	McLean, Johnson	??	1 Nov 1785	Fredricksburgh		Croton River; Swift, Josiah; ; Birdsall, James; Muddy Brook: Bridge, ; anoter; Wichell, Timothy; Rocks, ledge; and Mountain,	
495	Robinson	Hyatt, John	316	7 Jul 1786	Phillips		Hollow, Hemlock; Fredricksburgh Line; Hyatt & Penier; Platt & Bailey; Saterly, Richard : Beverdam Brook; Christian, Richard ; and Hyatt & Co.	

Maps of Confiscated Property

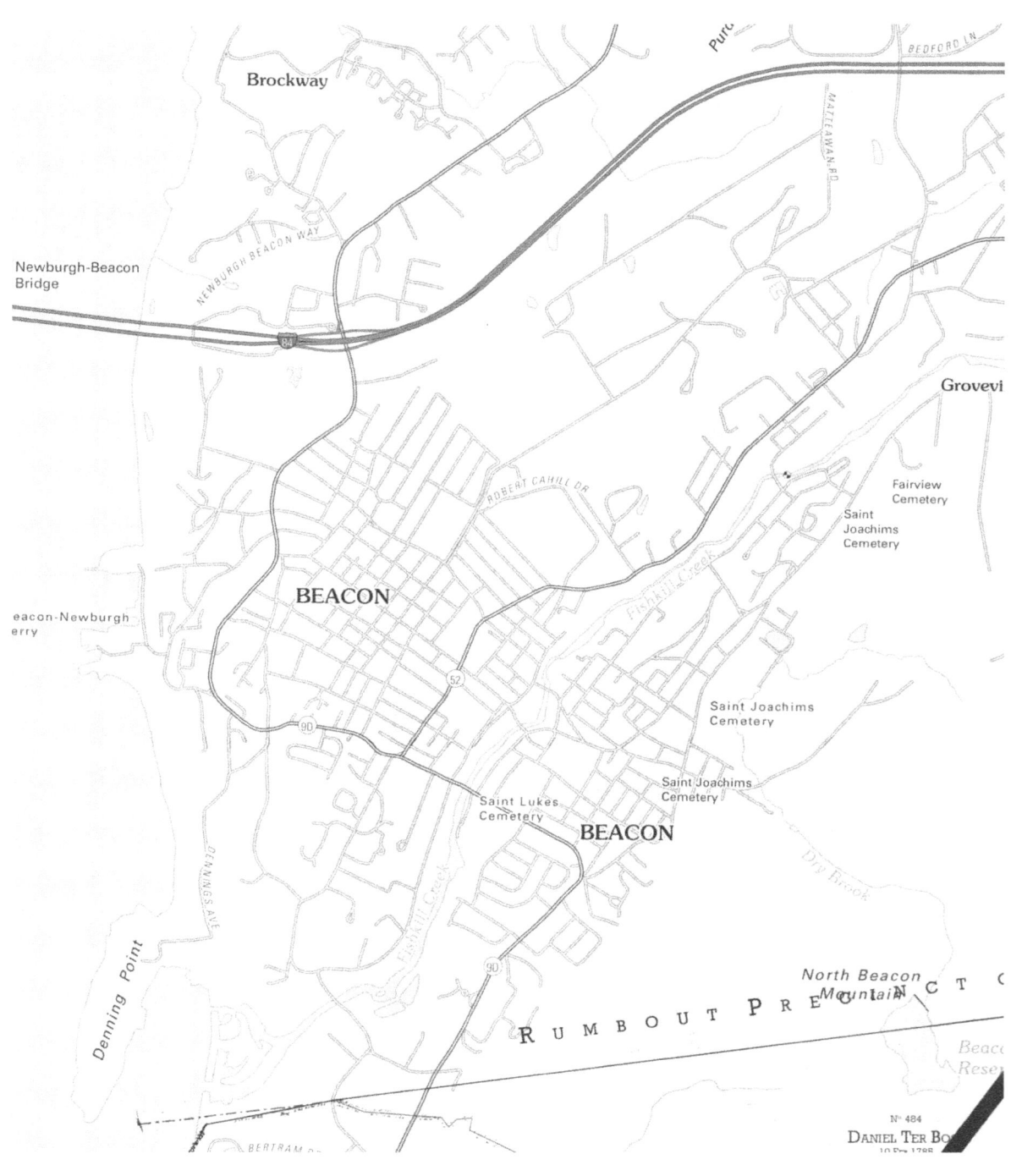

Confiscated Property of Philipse Highland Patent, Putnam County, N.Y
map continues on page 30

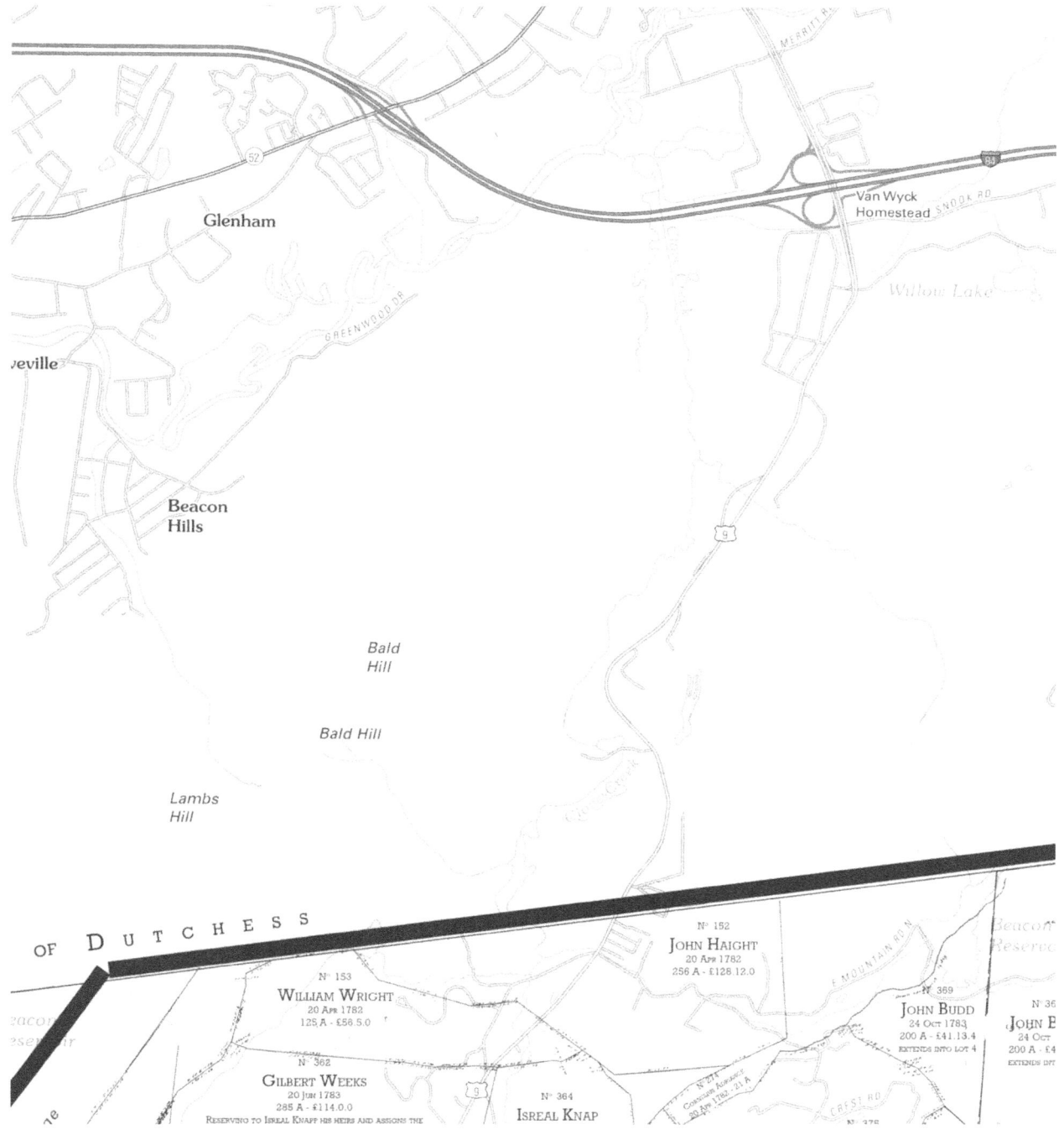

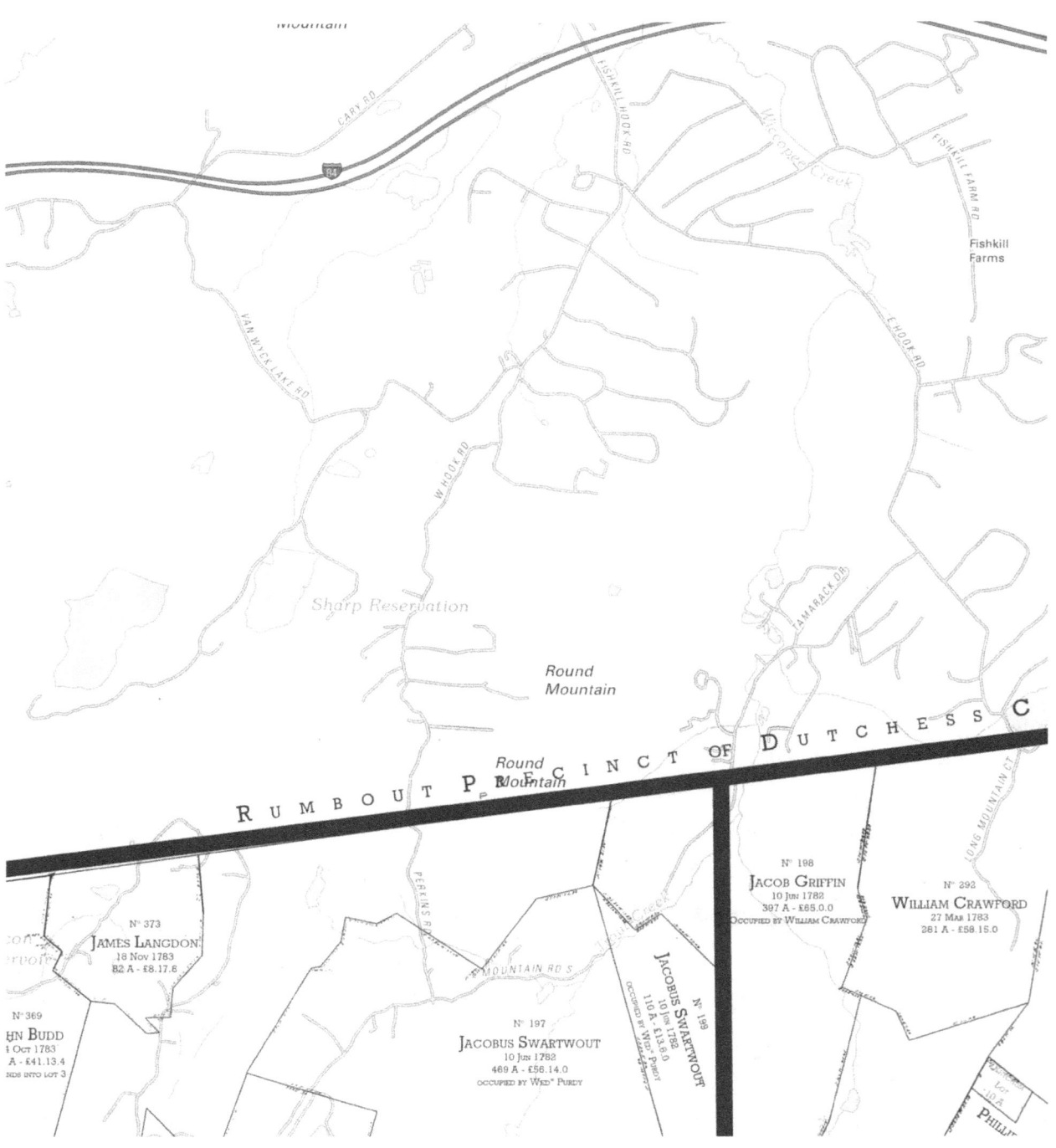

Confiscated Property of Philipse Highland Patent, Putnam County, N.Y

map continues on page 32

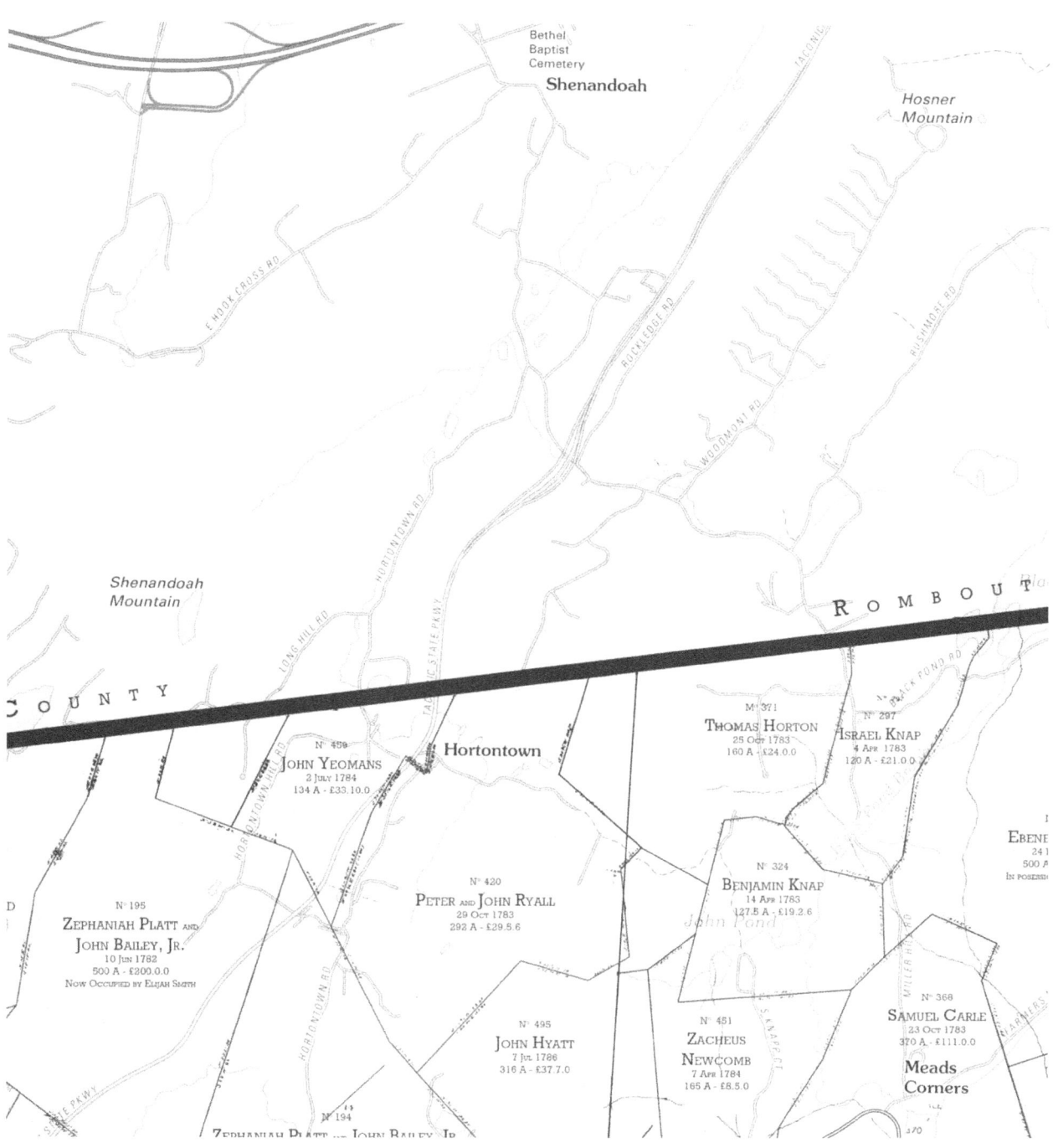

Confiscated Property of Philipse Highland Patent, Putnam County, N.Y
map continues on page 33

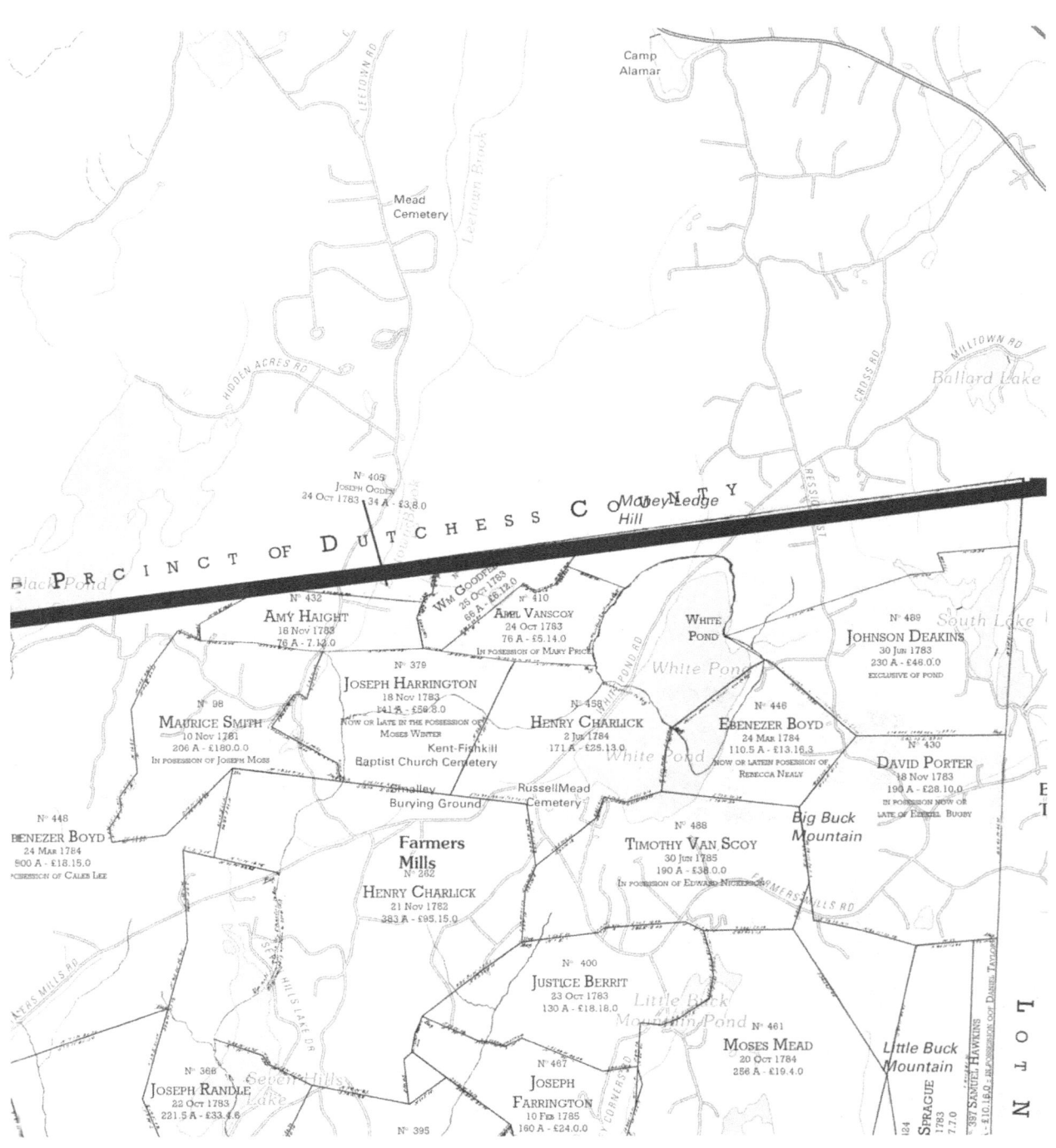

Confiscated Property of Philipse Highland Patent, Putnam County, N.Y
map continues on page 34

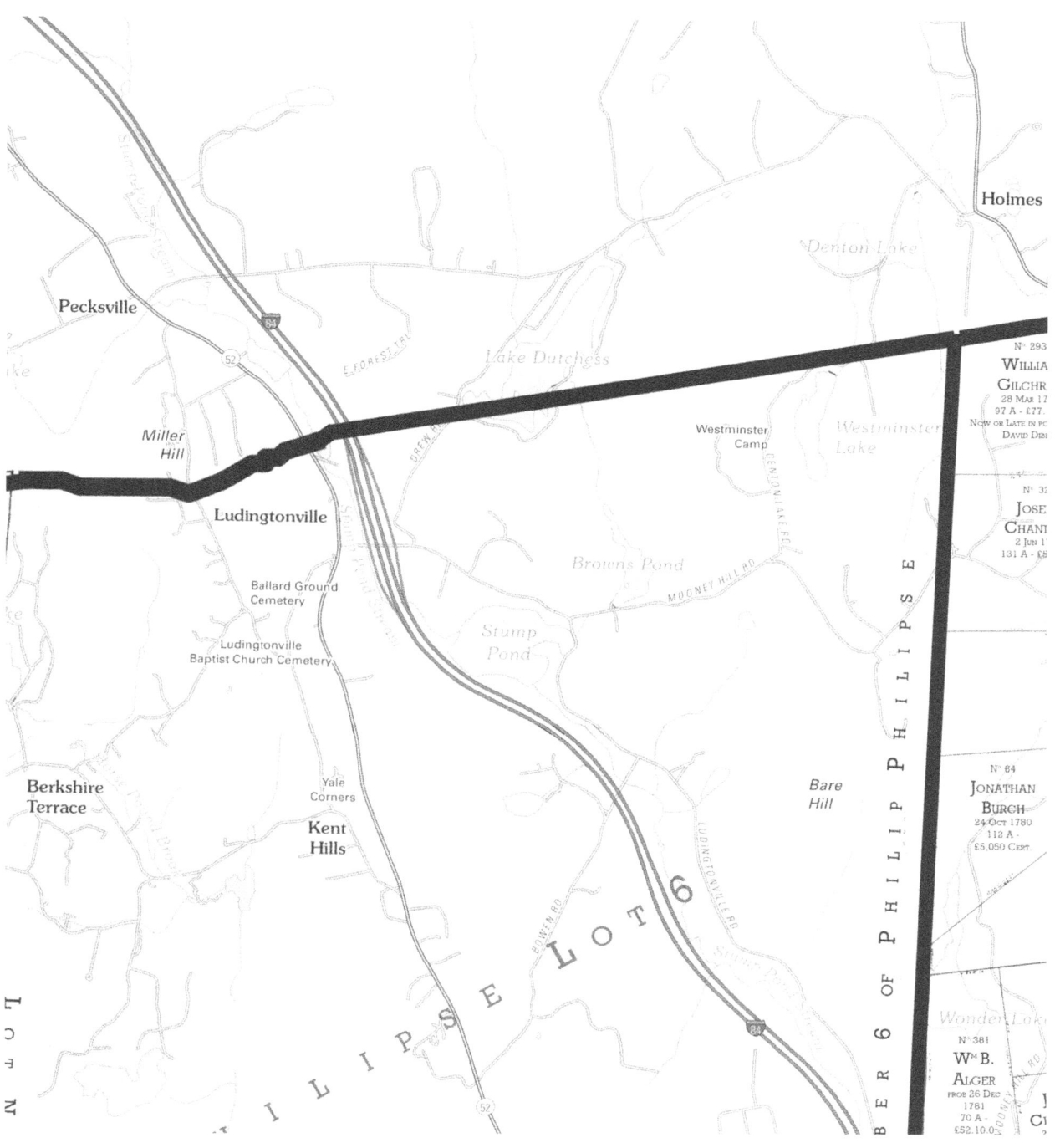

Confiscated Property of Philipse Highland Patent, Putnam County, N.Y
map continues on page 35

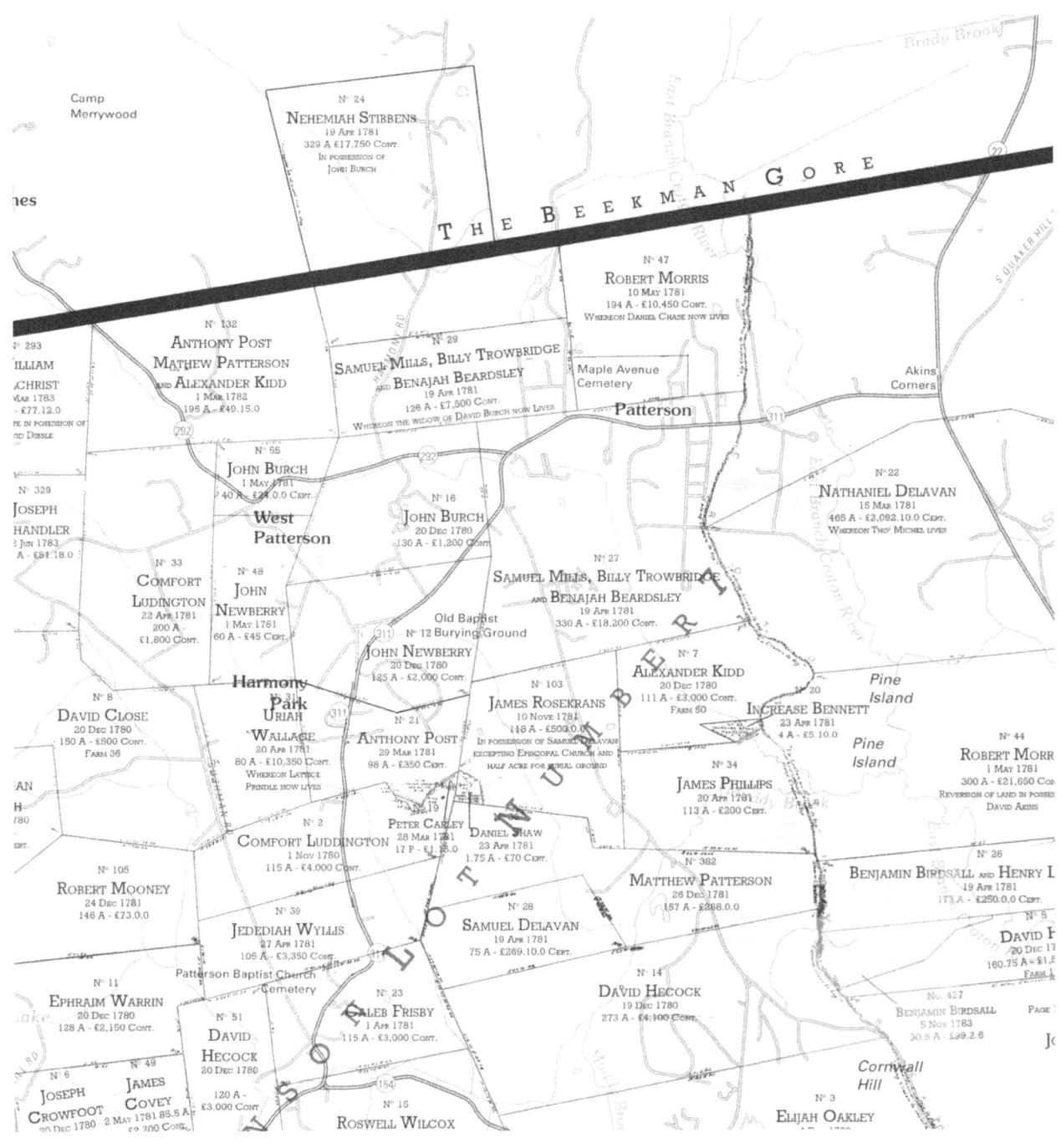

Confiscated Property of Philipse Highland Patent, Putnam County, N.Y
map continues on page 36

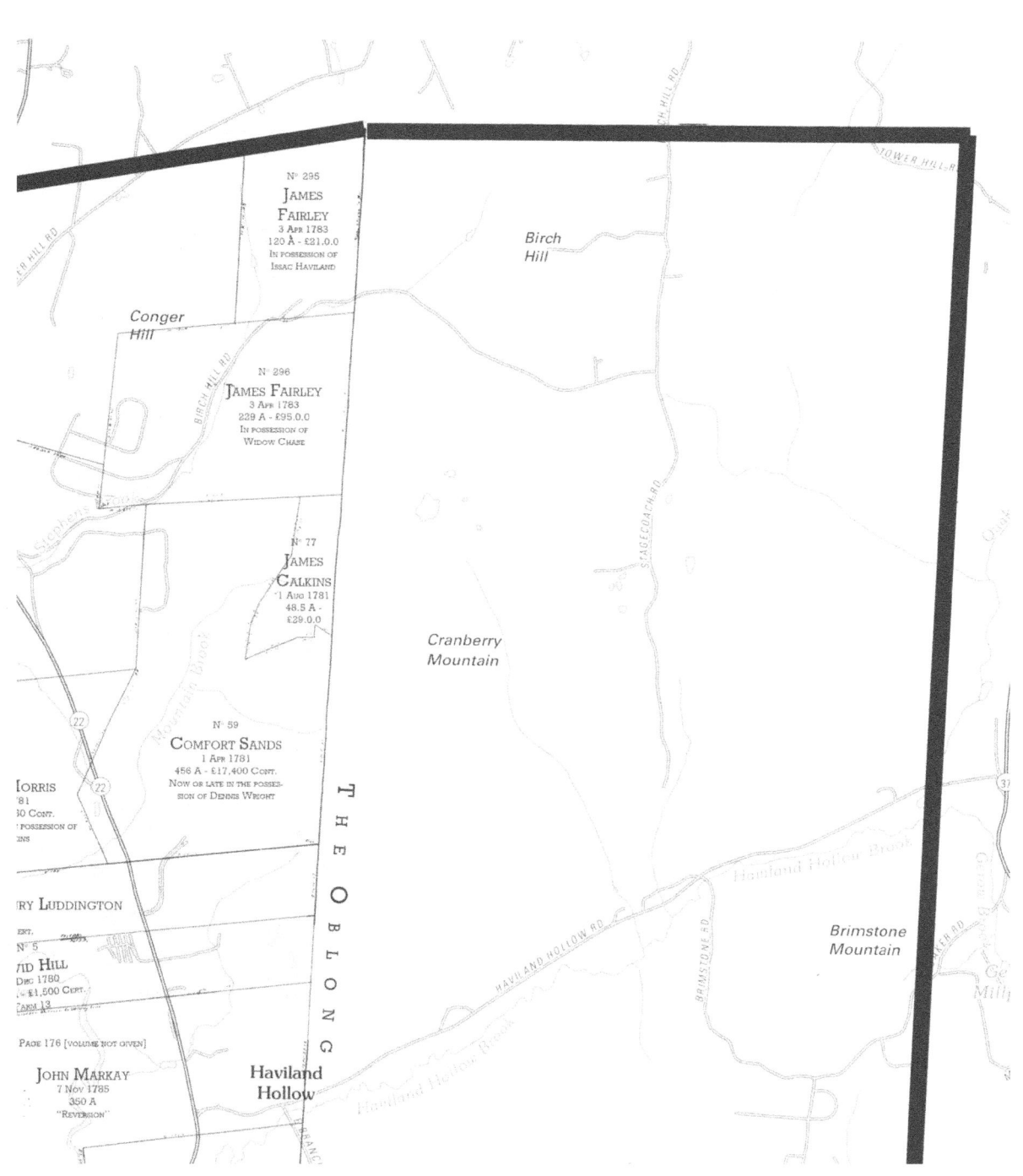

Confiscated Property of Philipse Highland Patent, Putnam County, N.Y
map continues on page 37

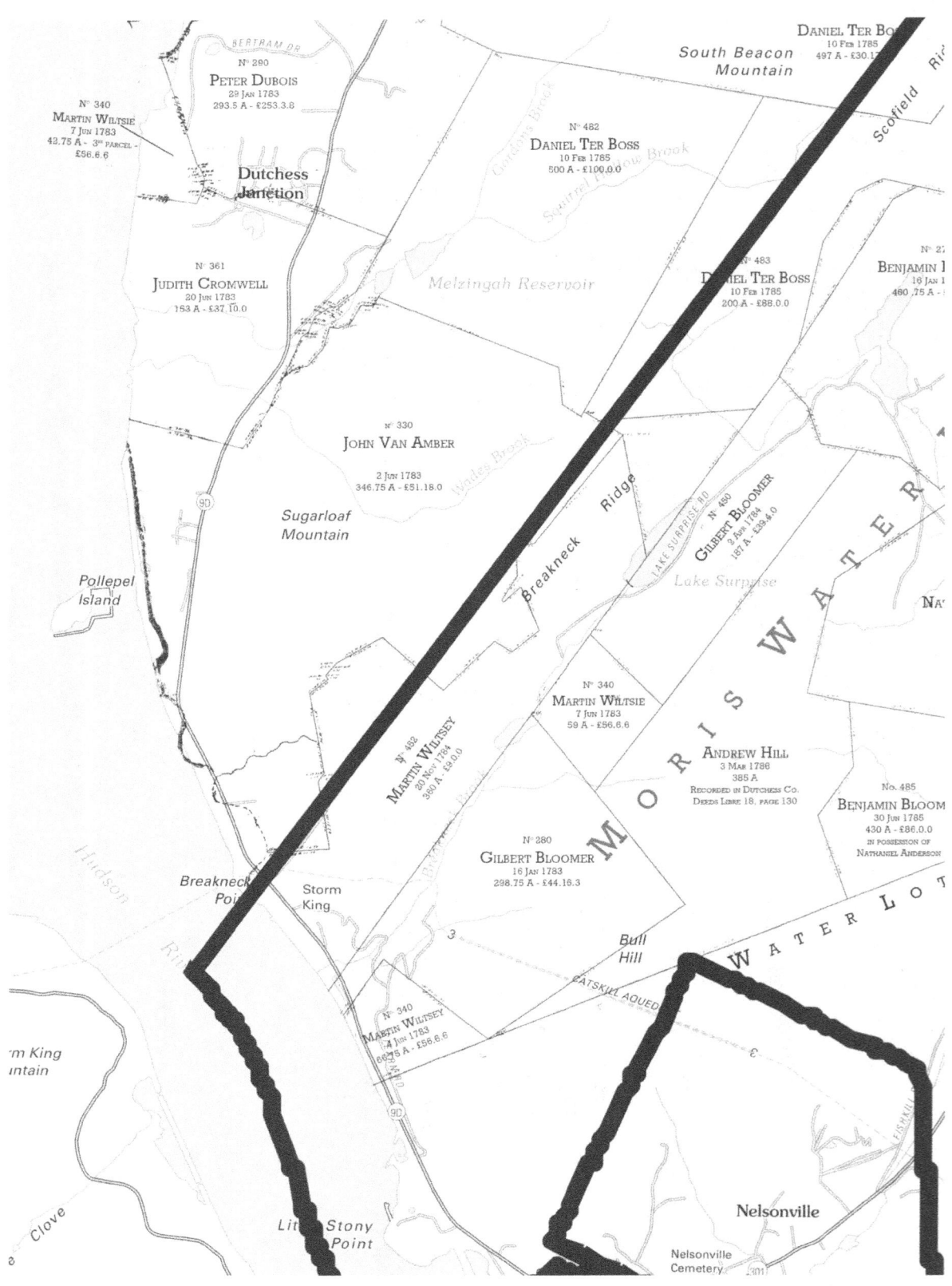

Confiscated Property of Philipse Highland Patent, Putnam County, N.Y

map continues on page 23

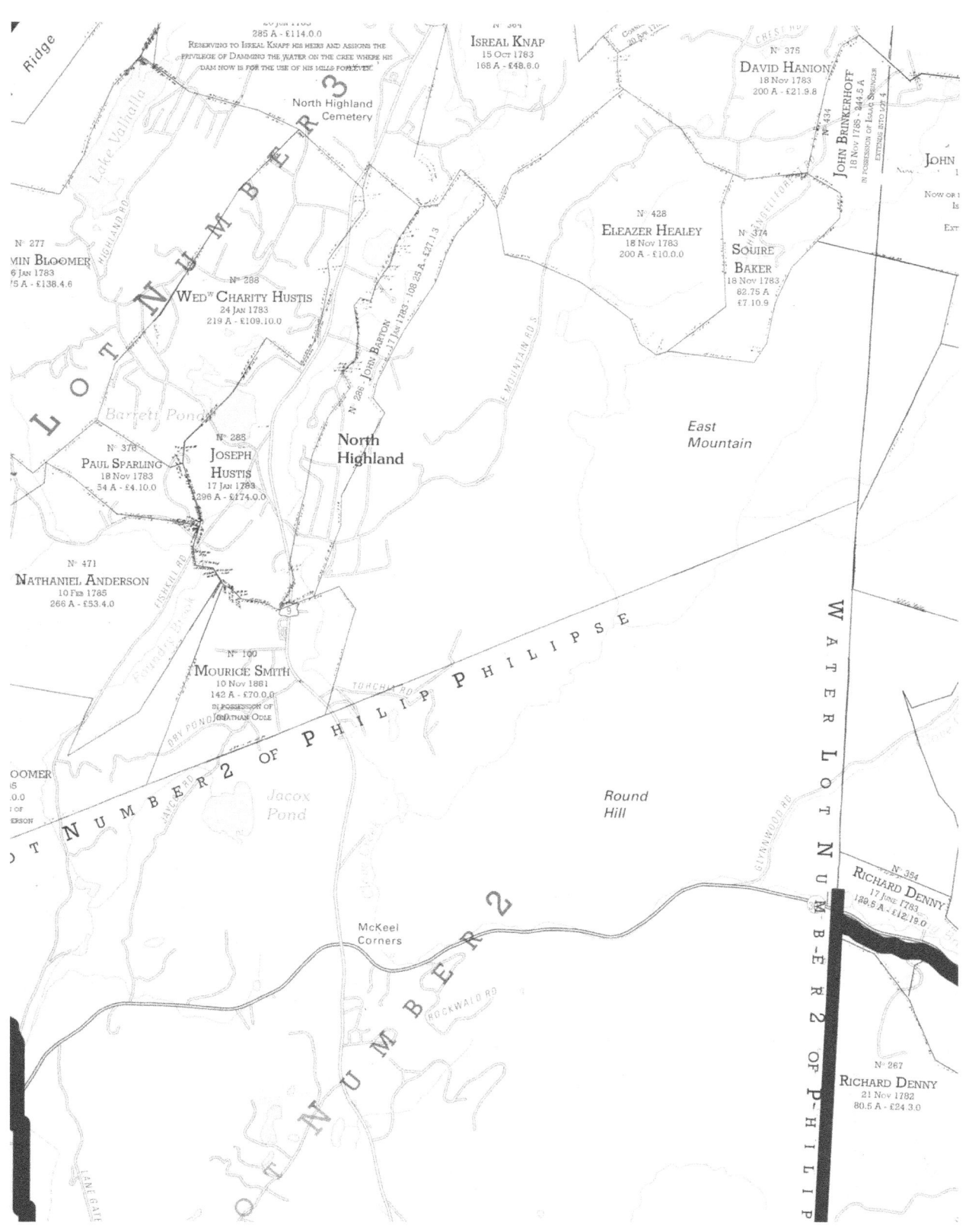

map continues on page 39

map continues on page 24

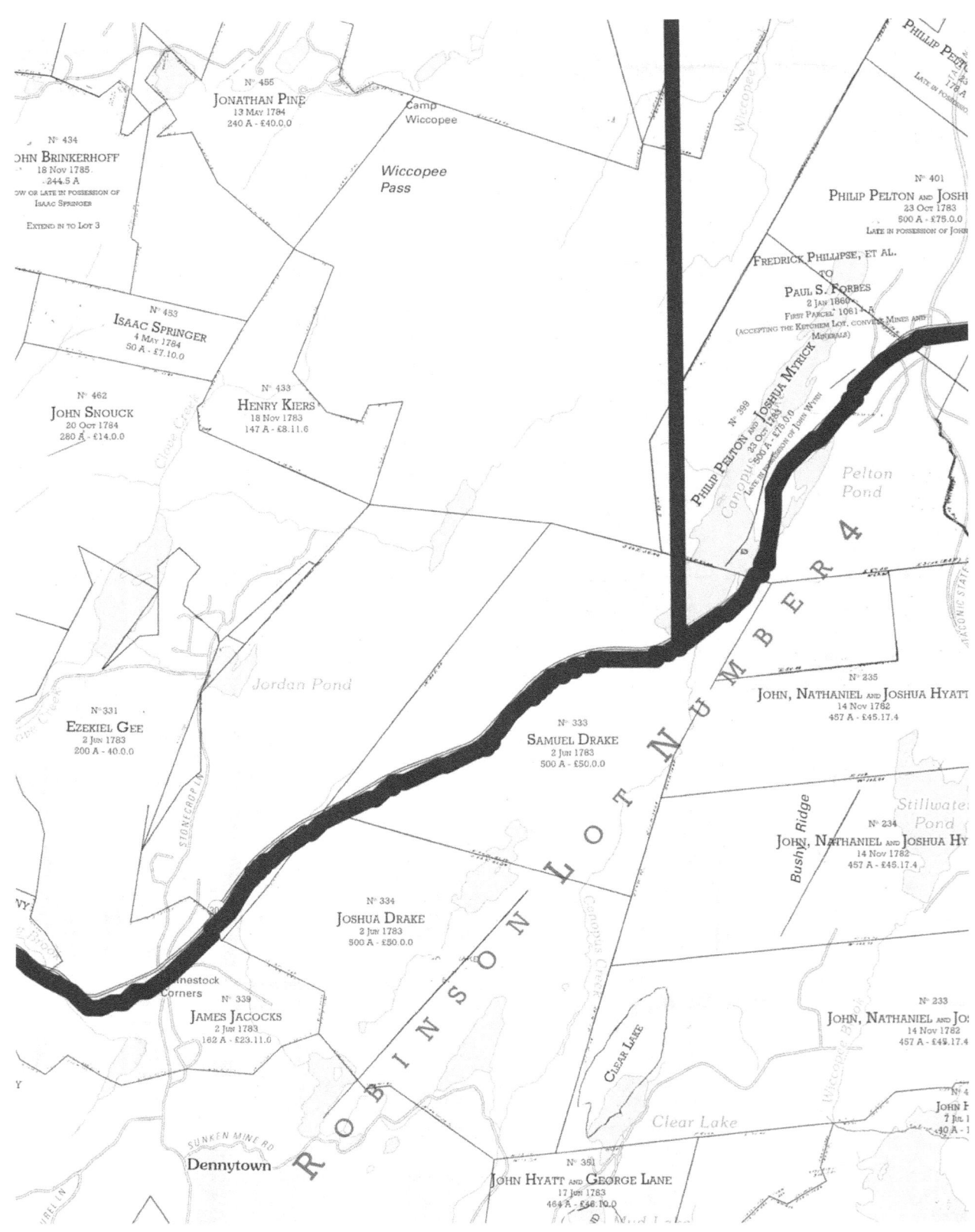

Confiscated Property of Philipse Highland Patent, Putnam County, N.Y

map continues on page 40

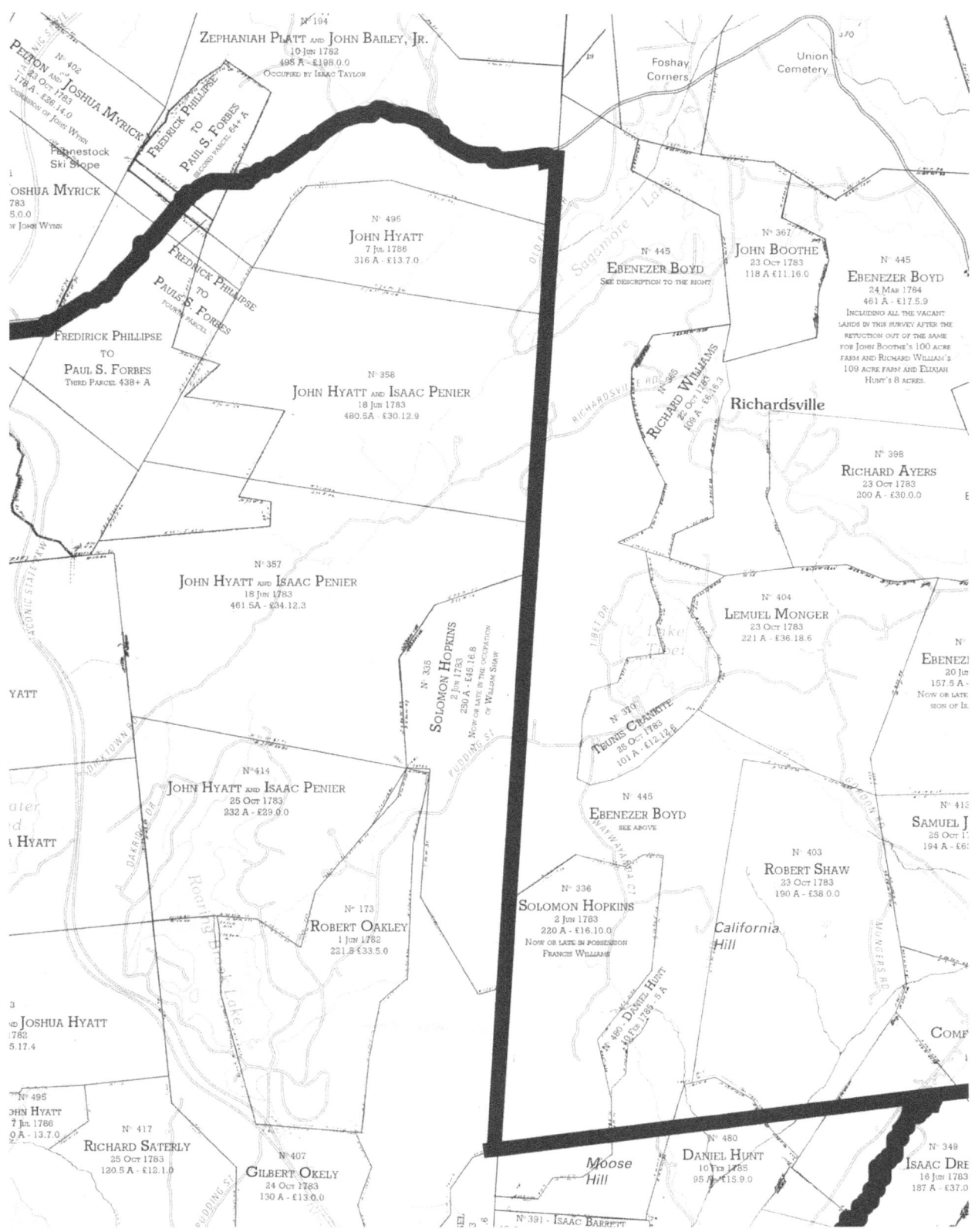

Confiscated Property of Philipse Highland Patent, Putnam County, N.Y

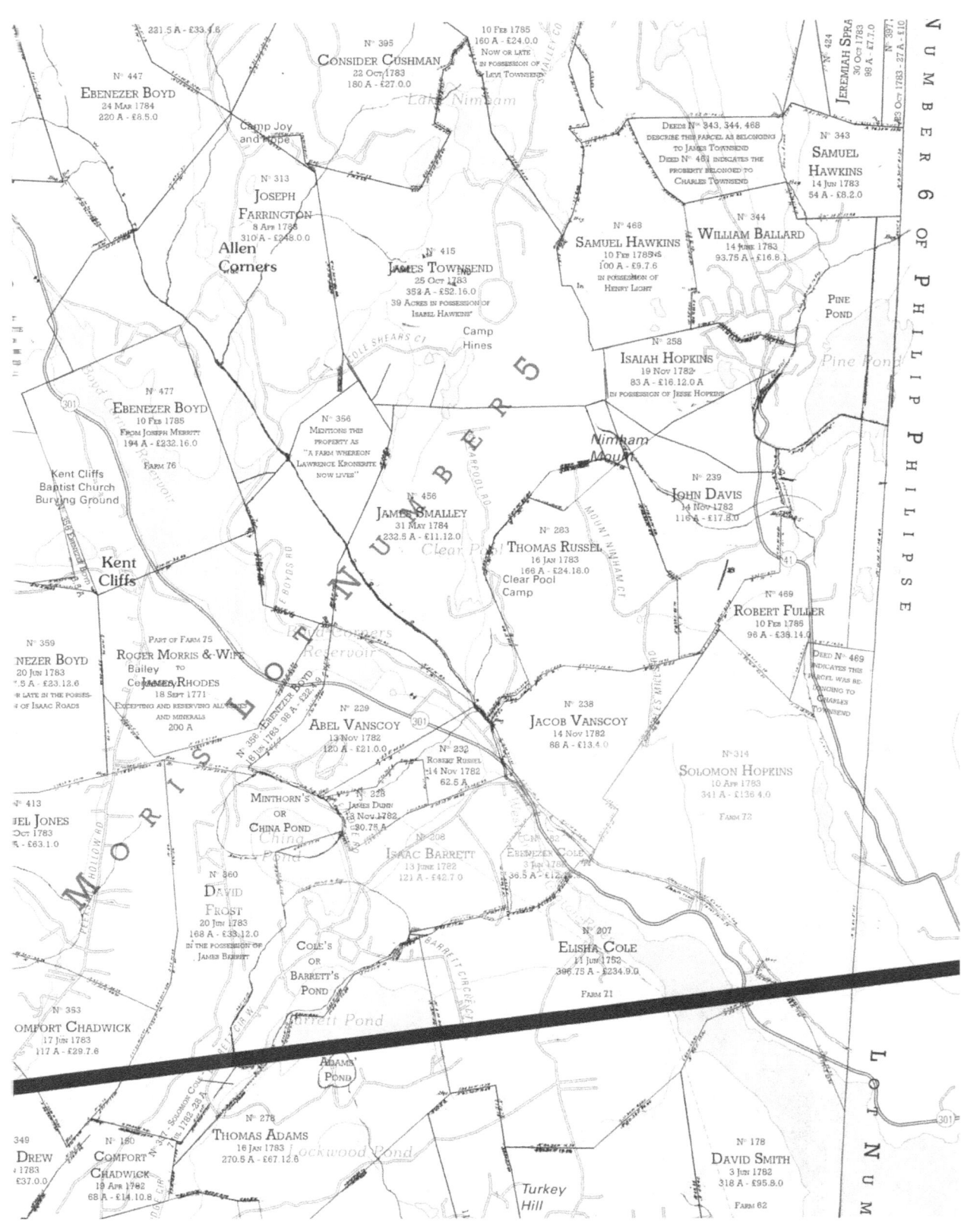

map continues on page 27

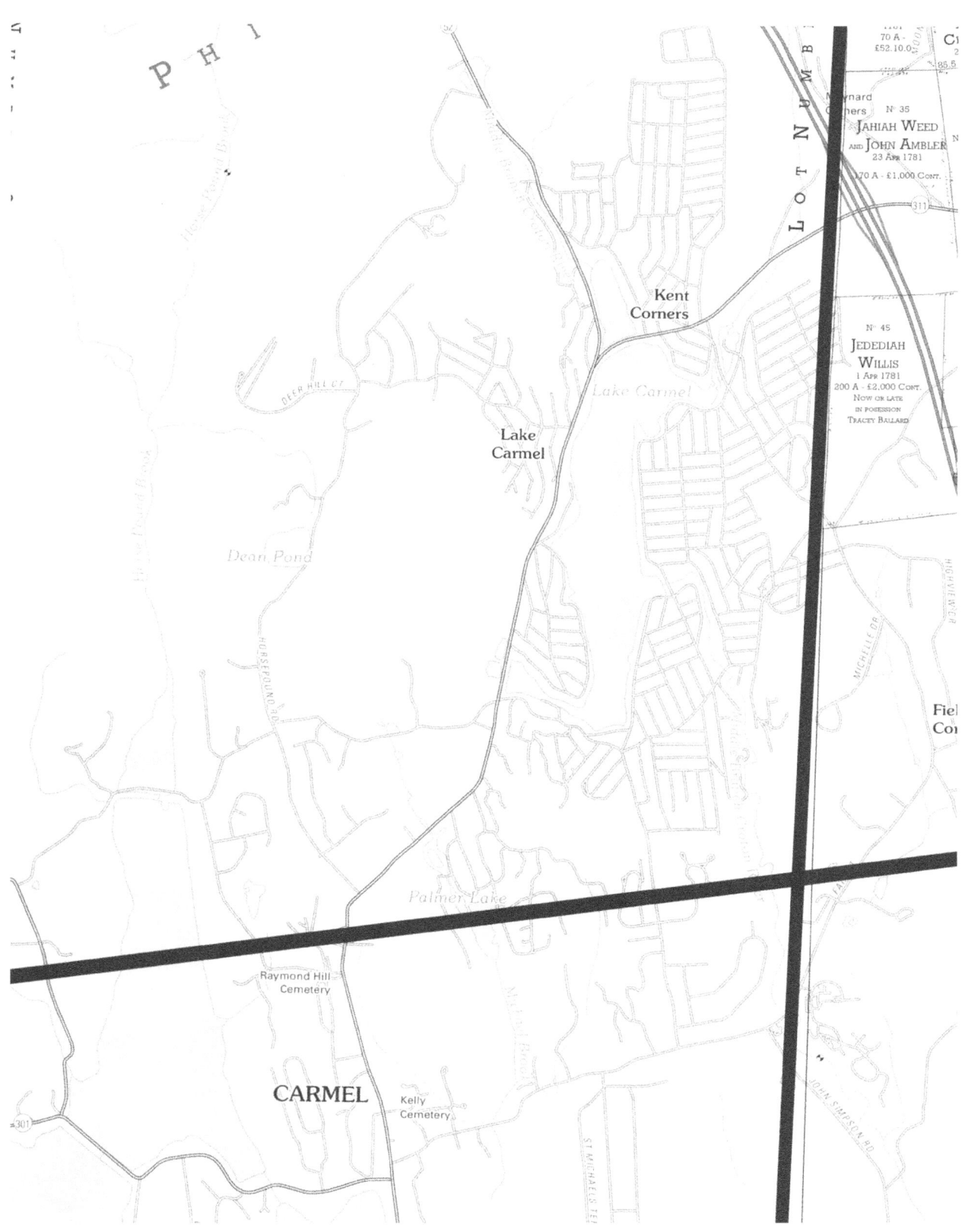

map continues on page 43

map continues on page 28

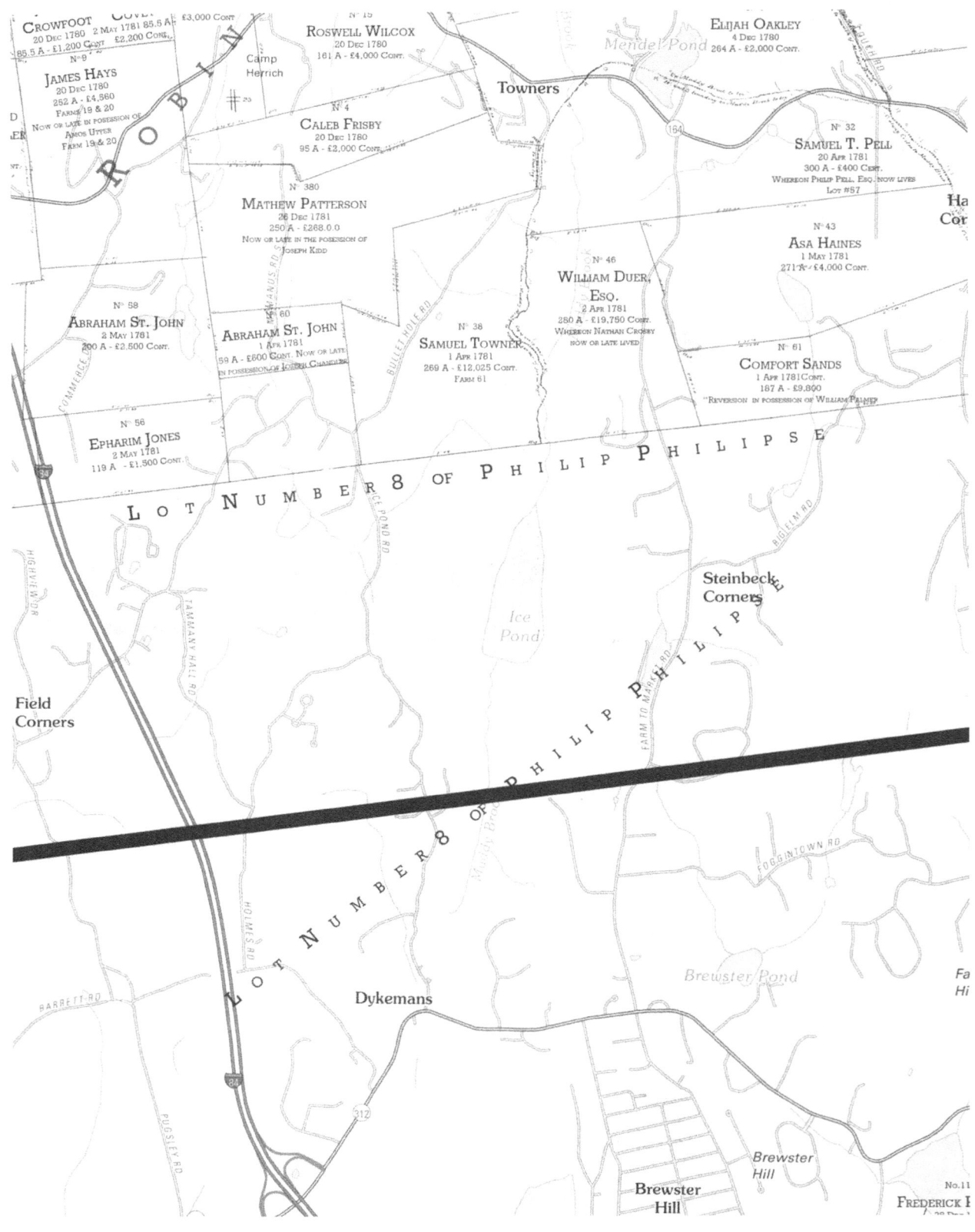

Confiscated Property of Philipse Highland Patent, Putnam County, N.Y

map continues on page 44

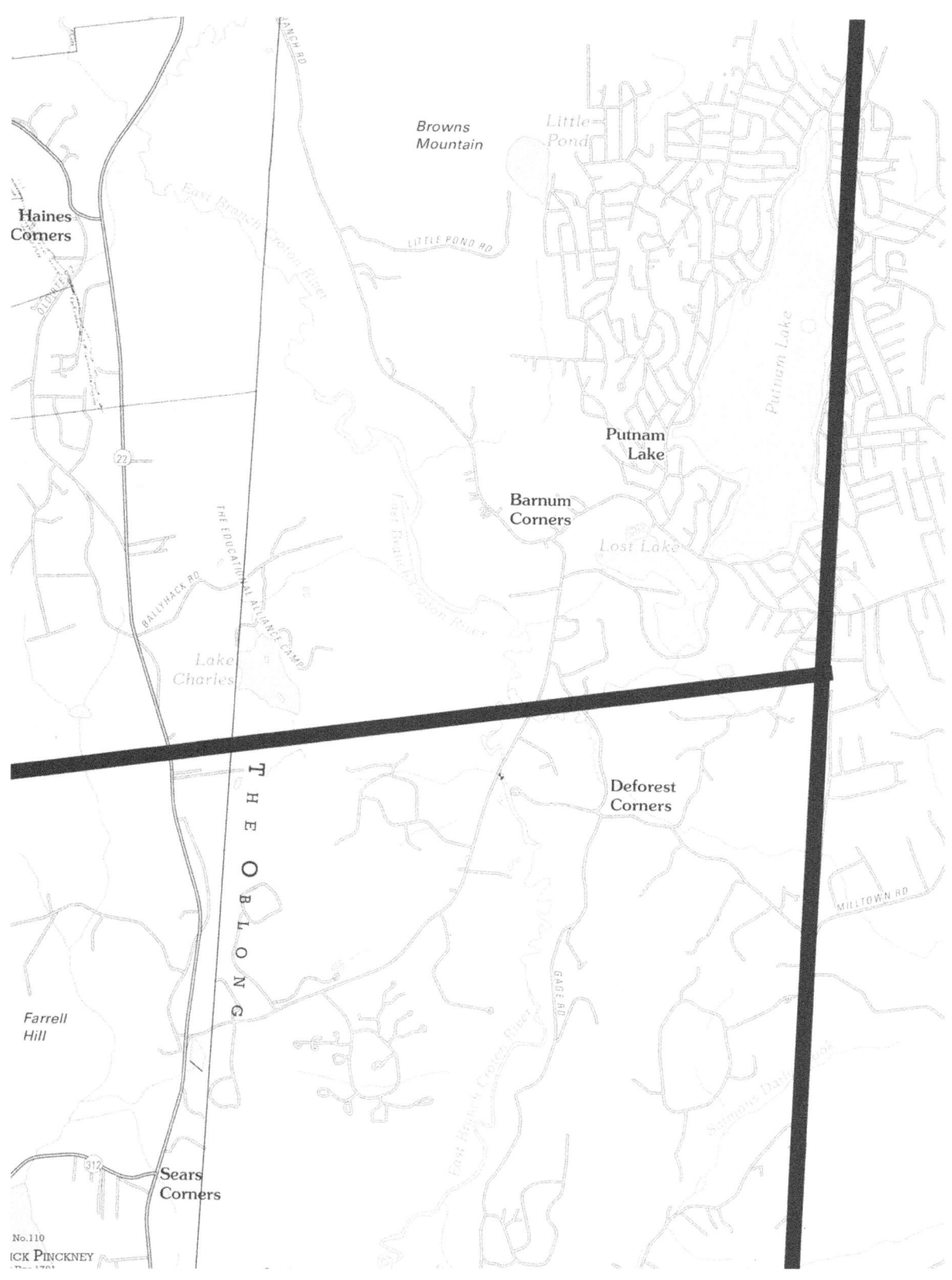

Confiscated Property of Philipse Highland Patent, Putnam County, N.Y
map continues on page 45

map continues on page 30

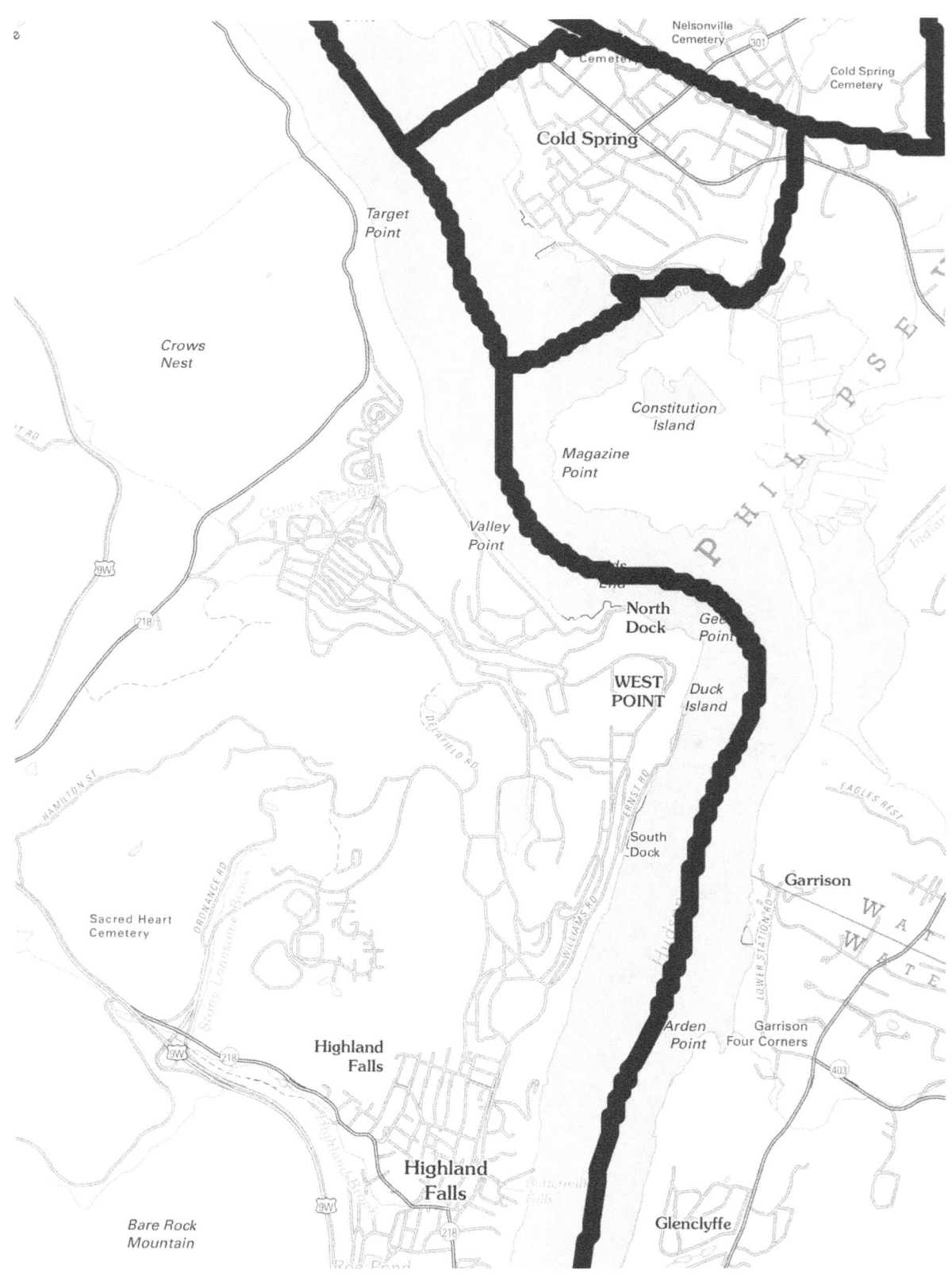

Confiscated Property of Philipse Highland Patent, Putnam County, N.Y
map continues on page 46

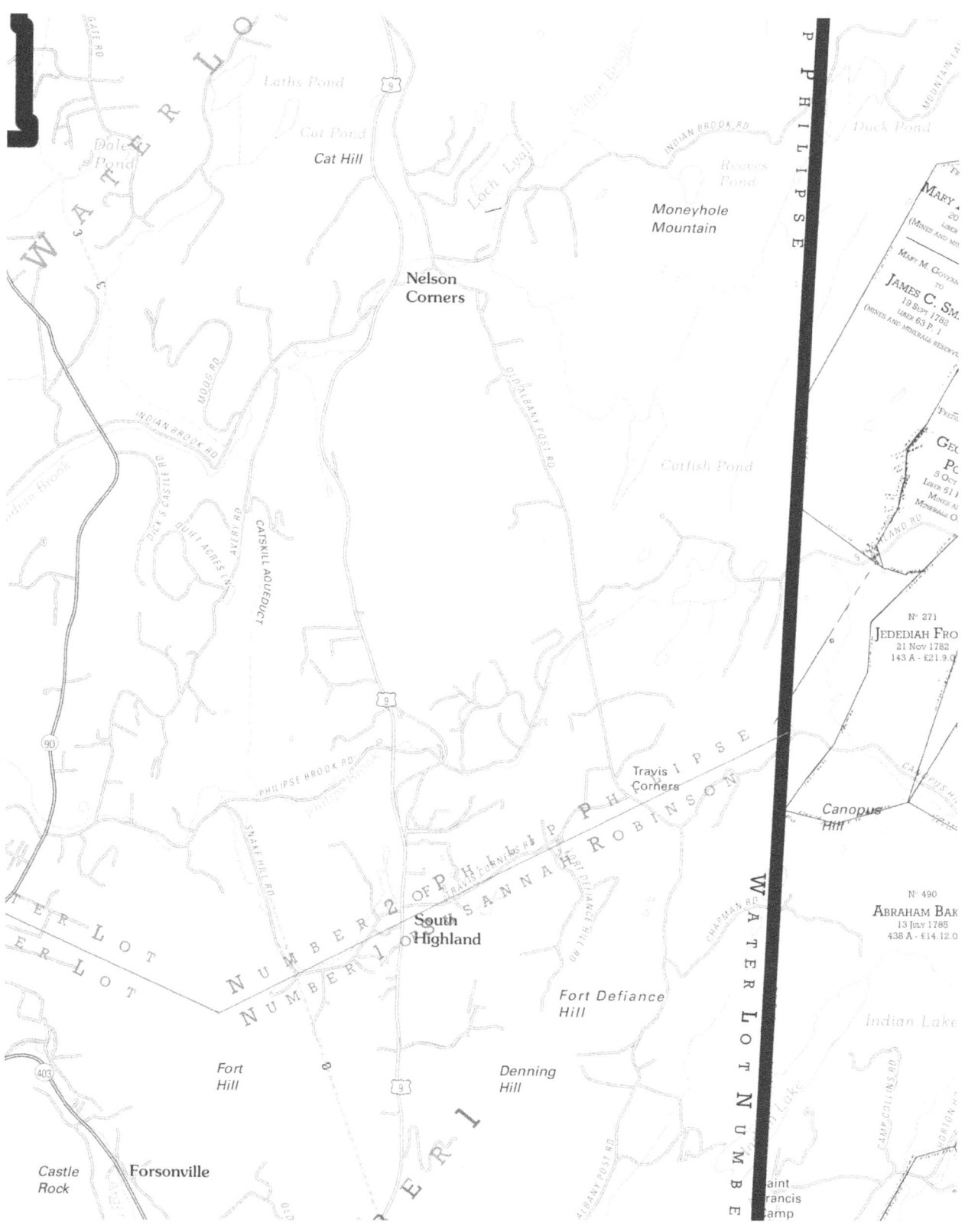

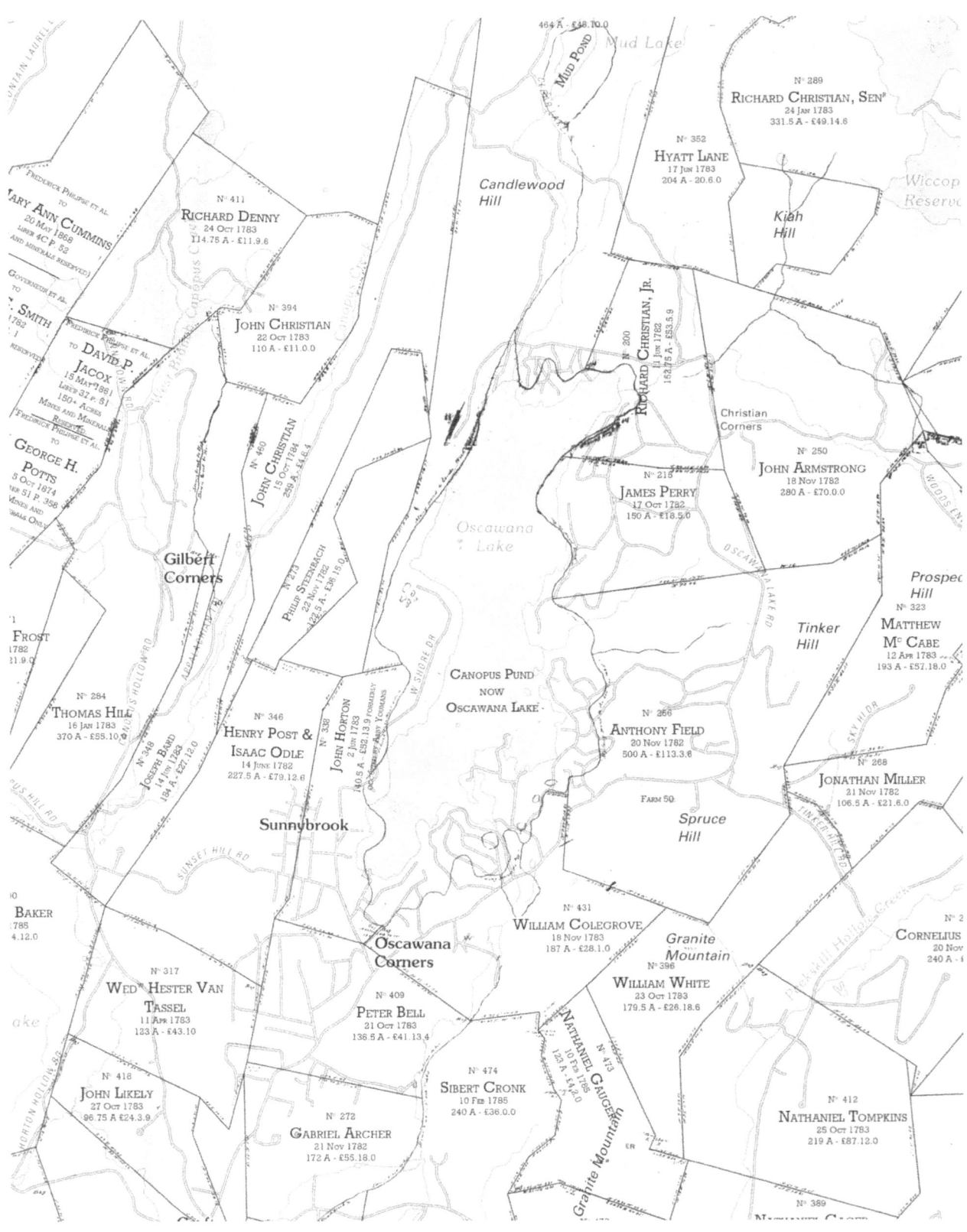

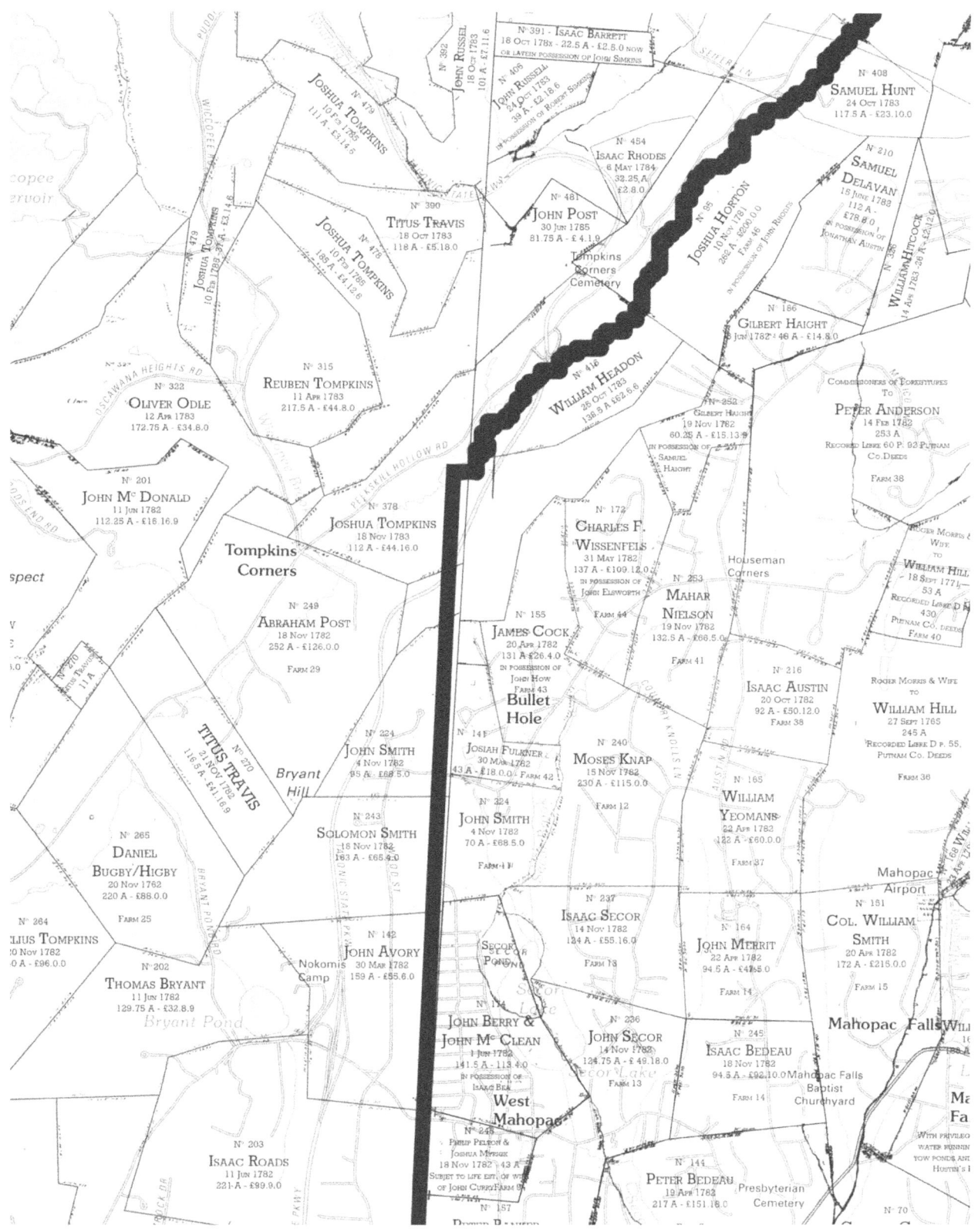

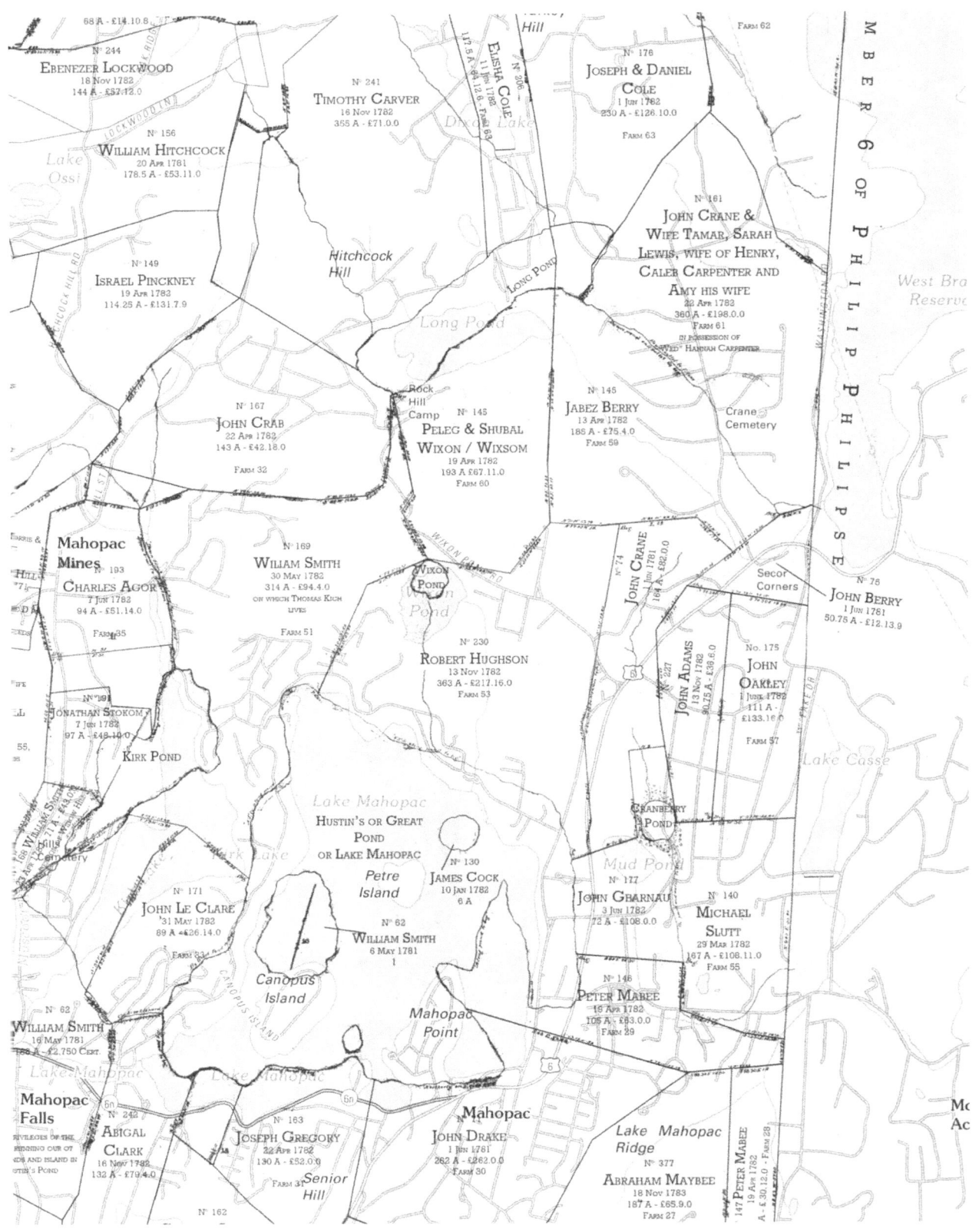

map continues on page 35

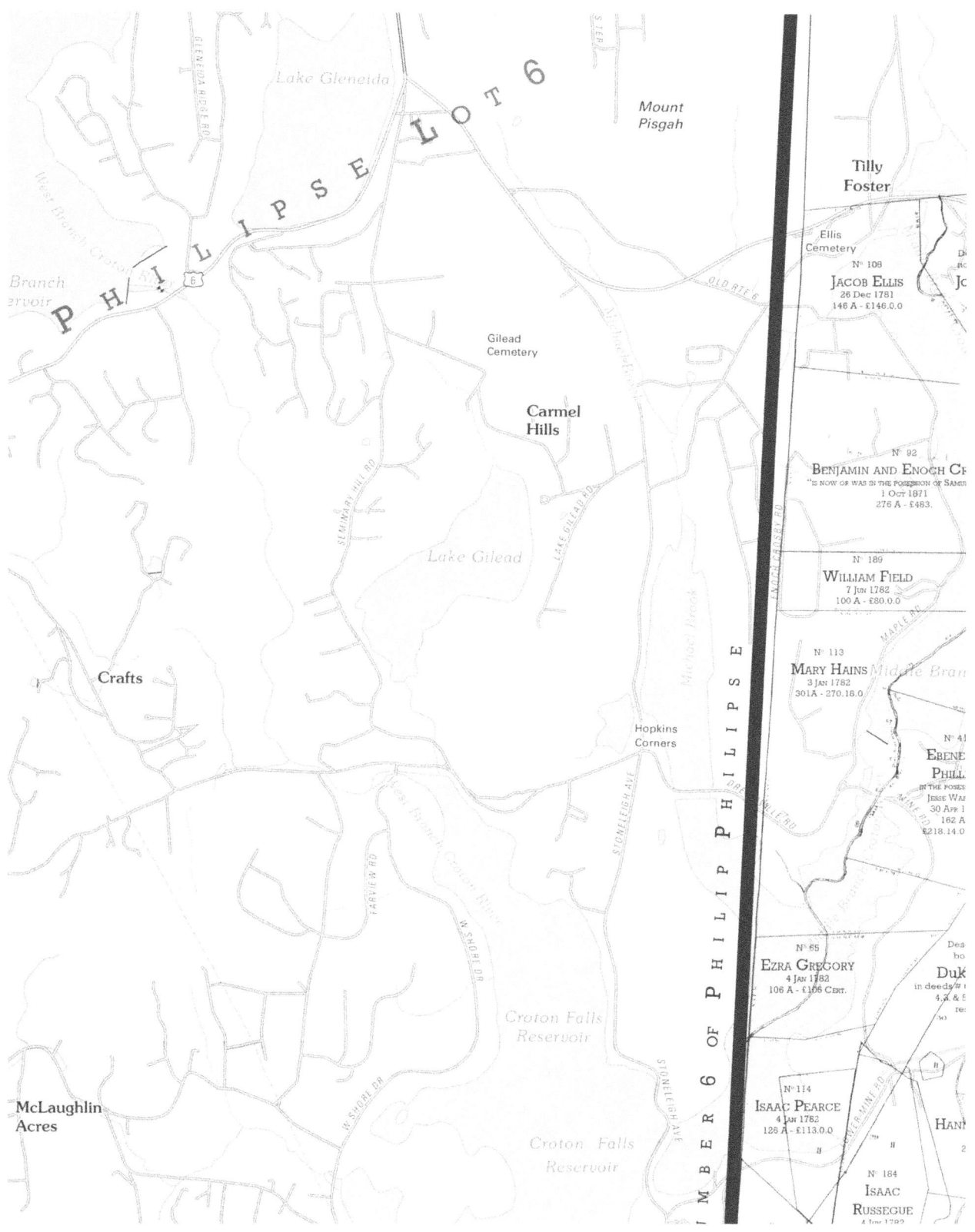

map continues on page 51

map continues on page 36

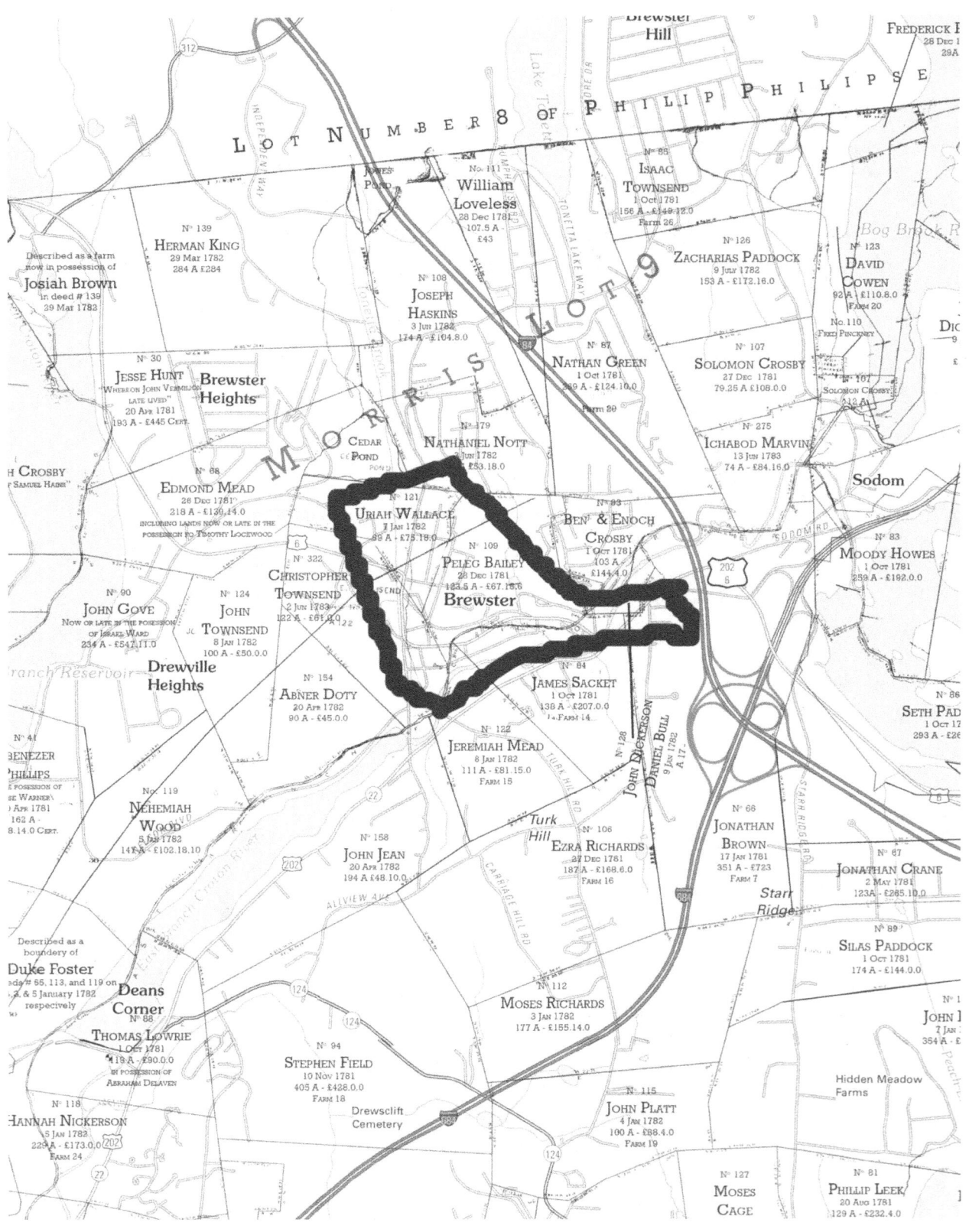

Confiscated Property of Philipse Highland Patent, Putnam County, N.Y

map continues on page 52

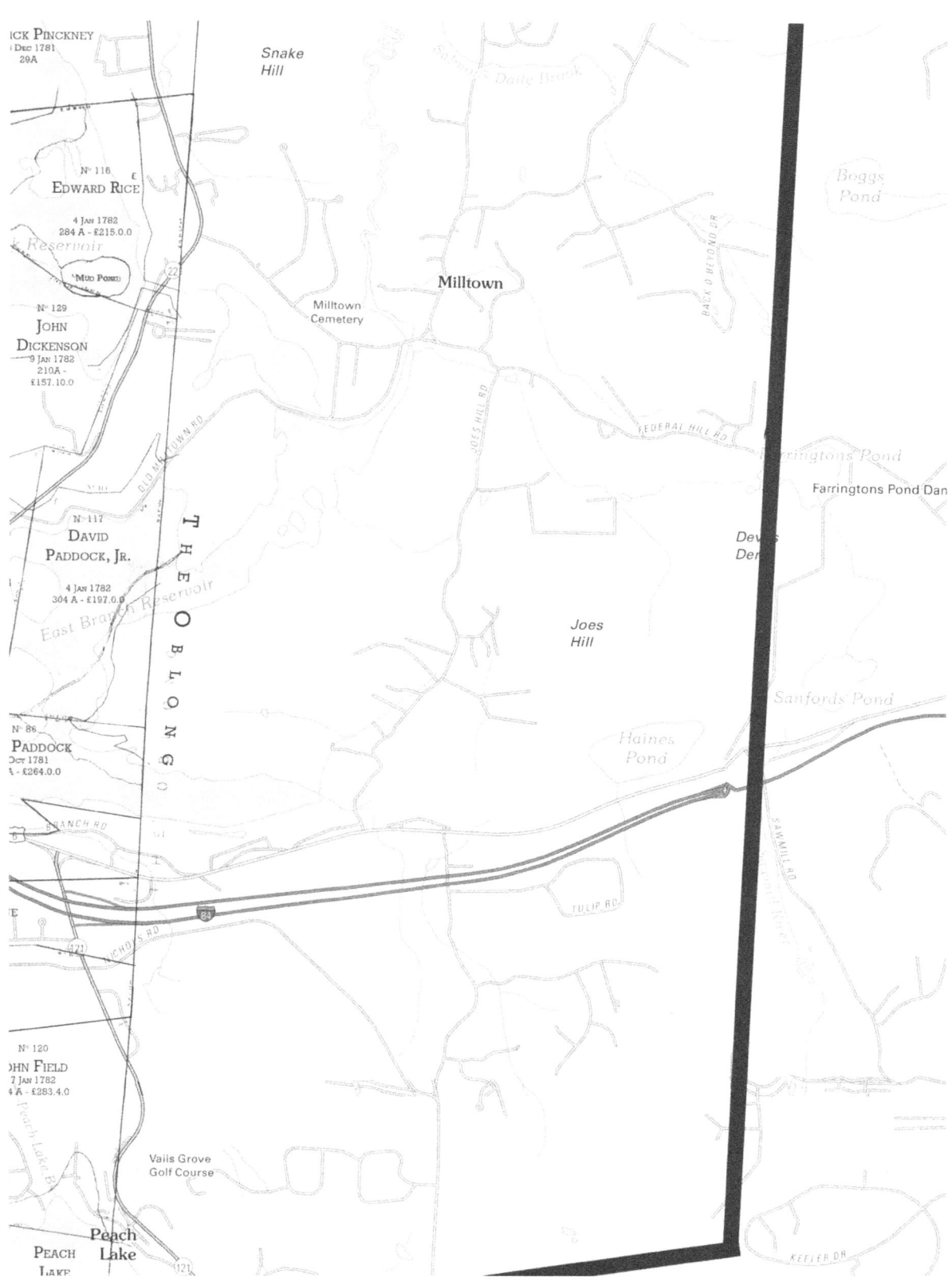

Confiscated Property of Philipse Highland Patent, Putnam County, N.Y.

map continues on page 38

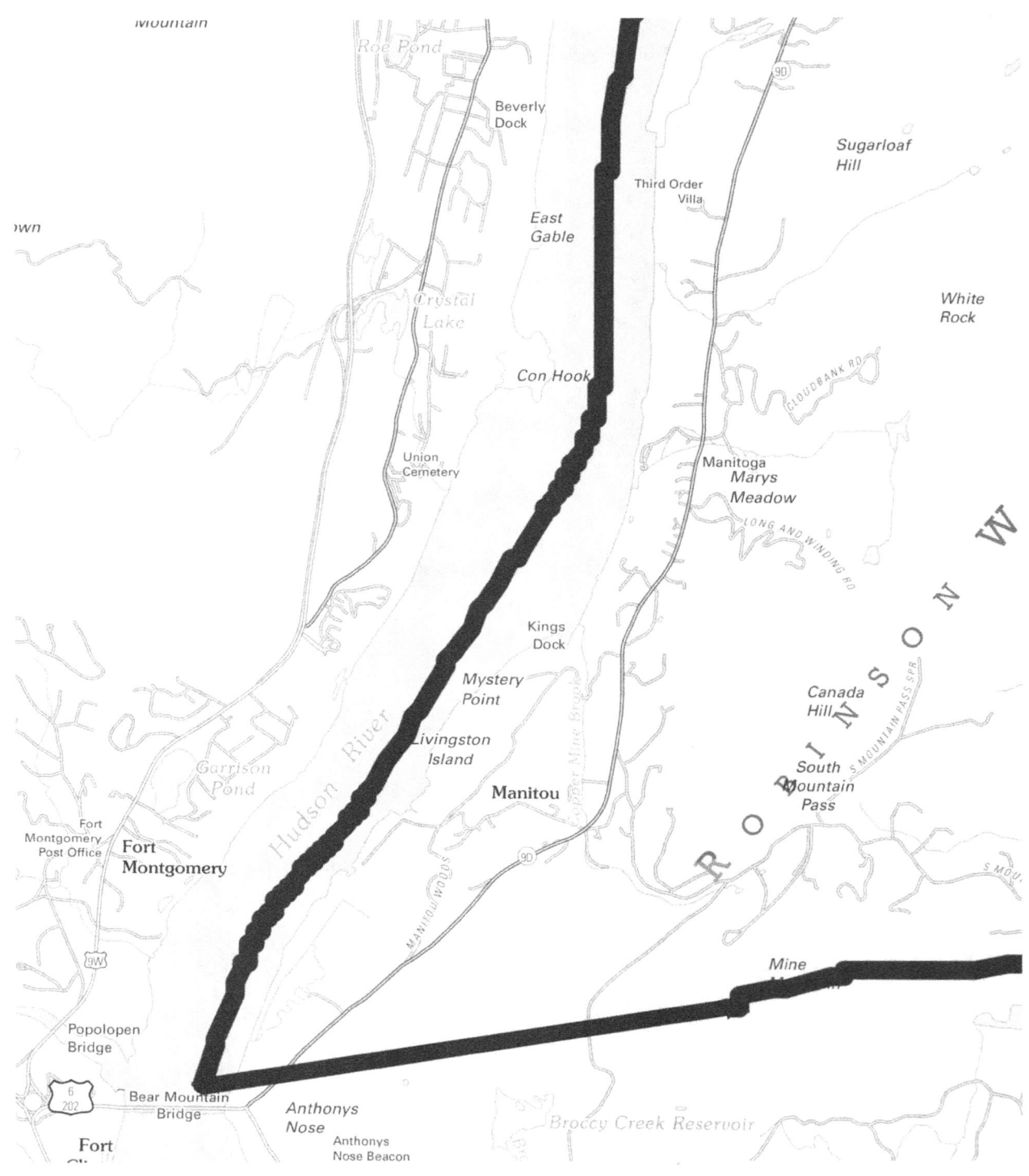

46   Confiscated Property of Philipse Highland Patent, Putnam County, N.Y

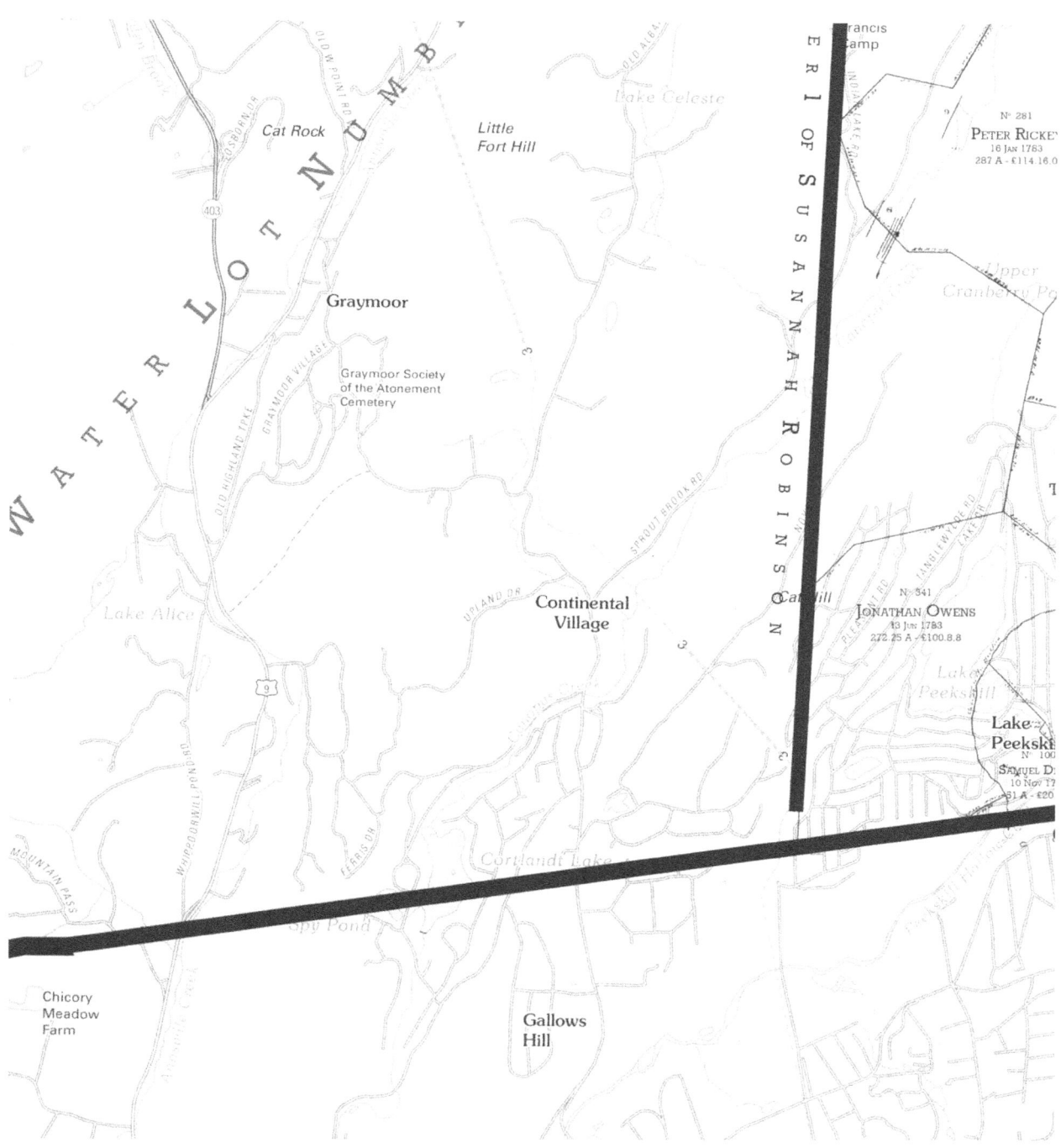

map continues on page 40

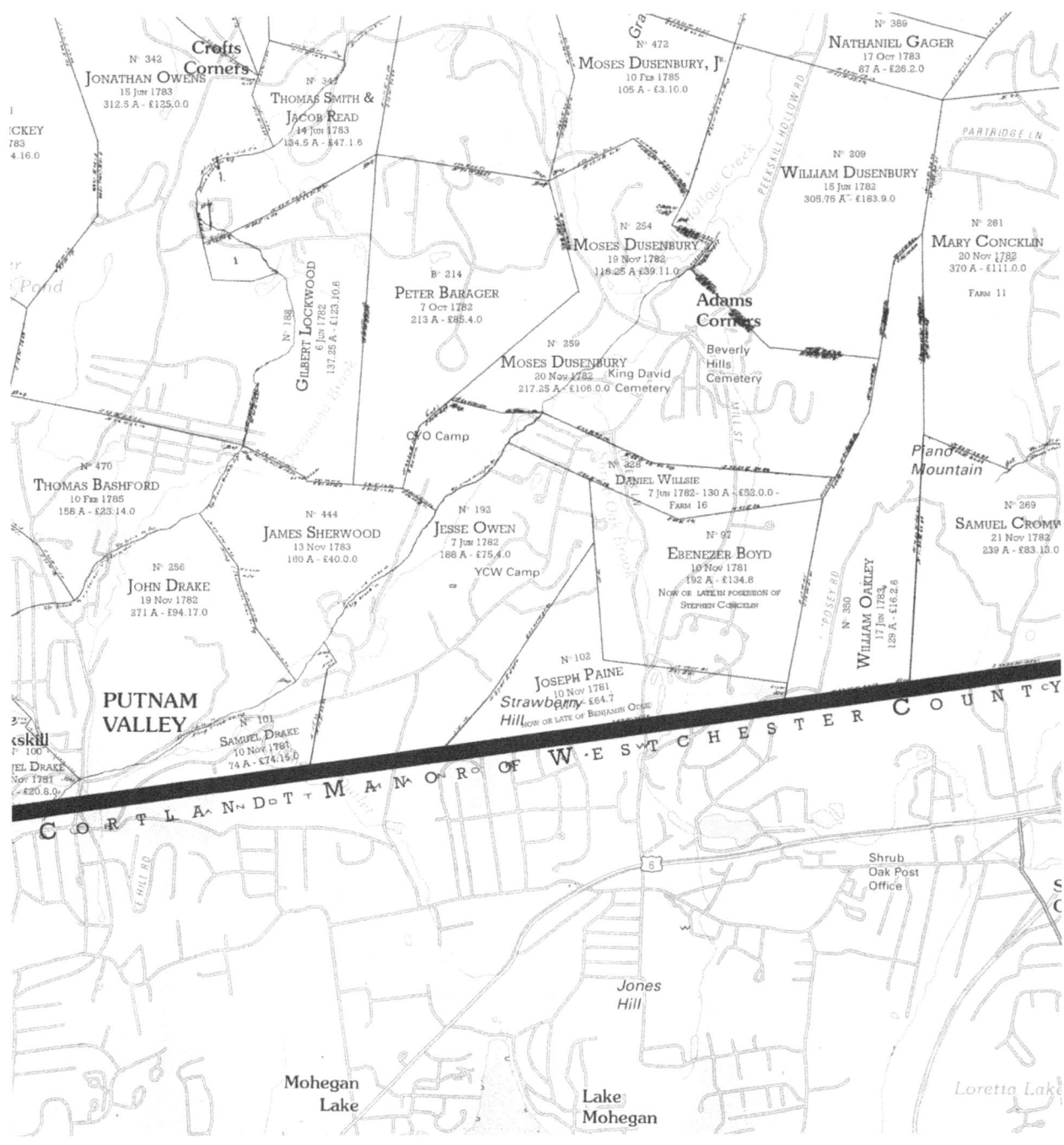

map continues on page 41

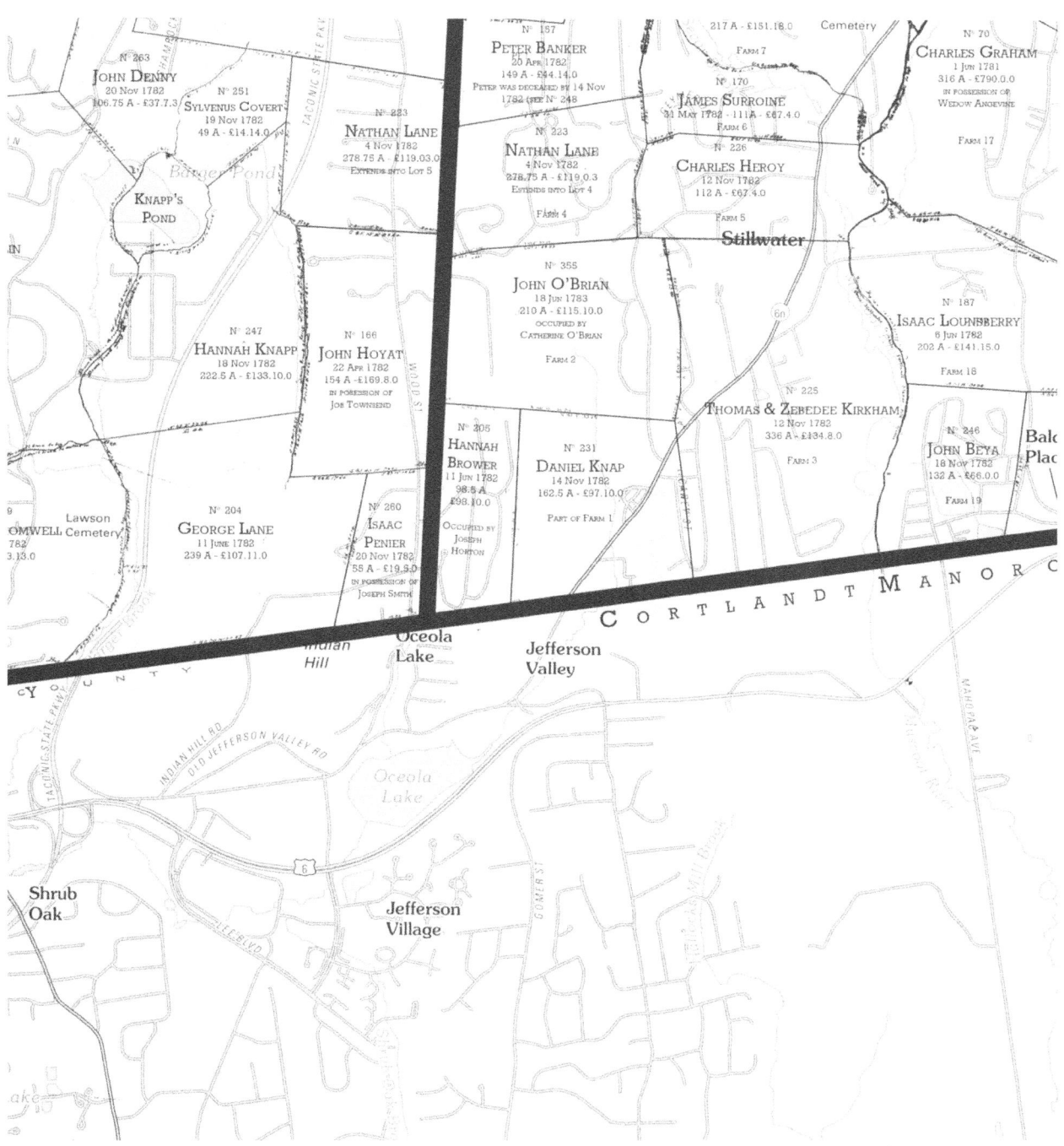

map continues on page 42

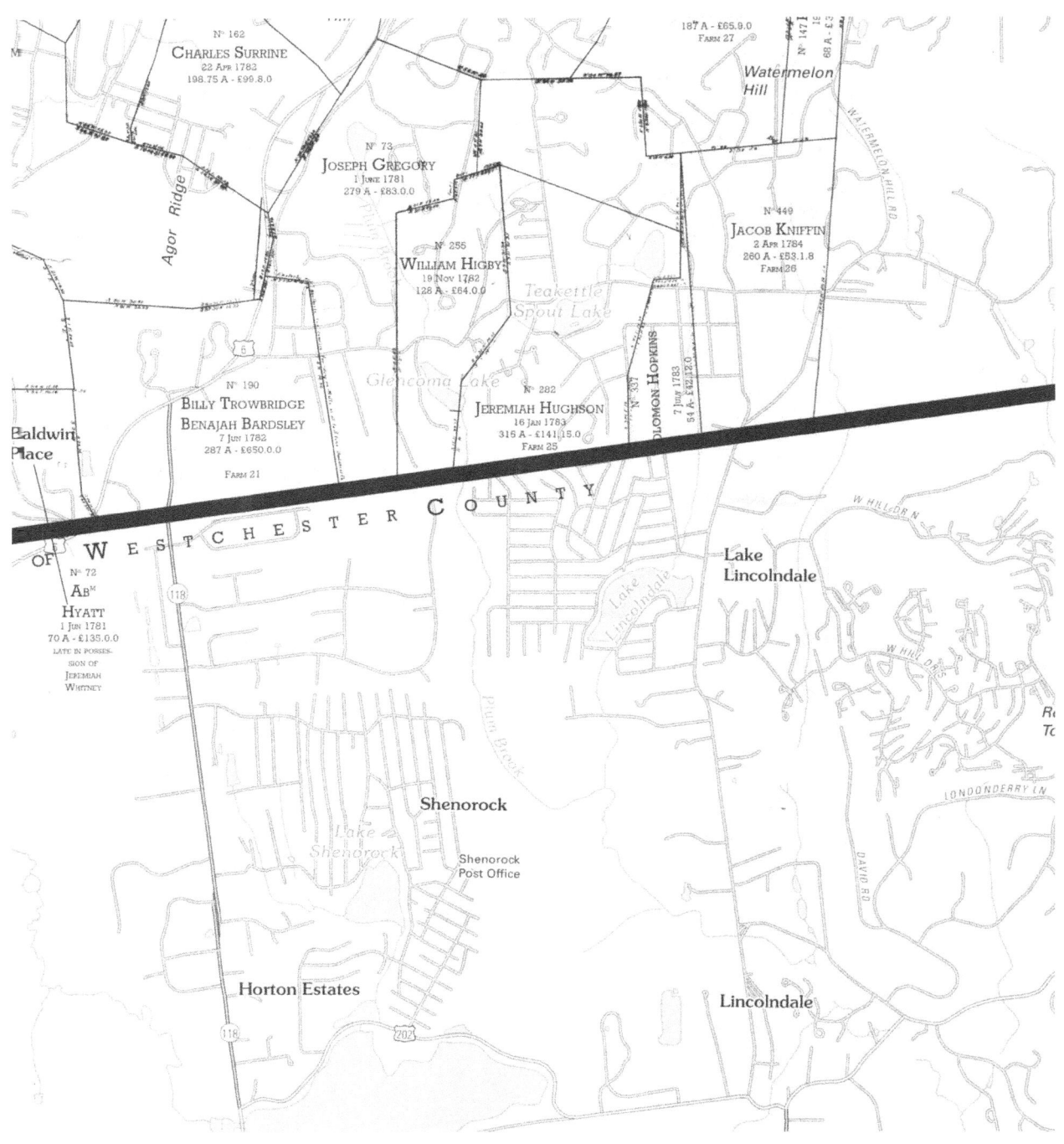

map continues on page 43

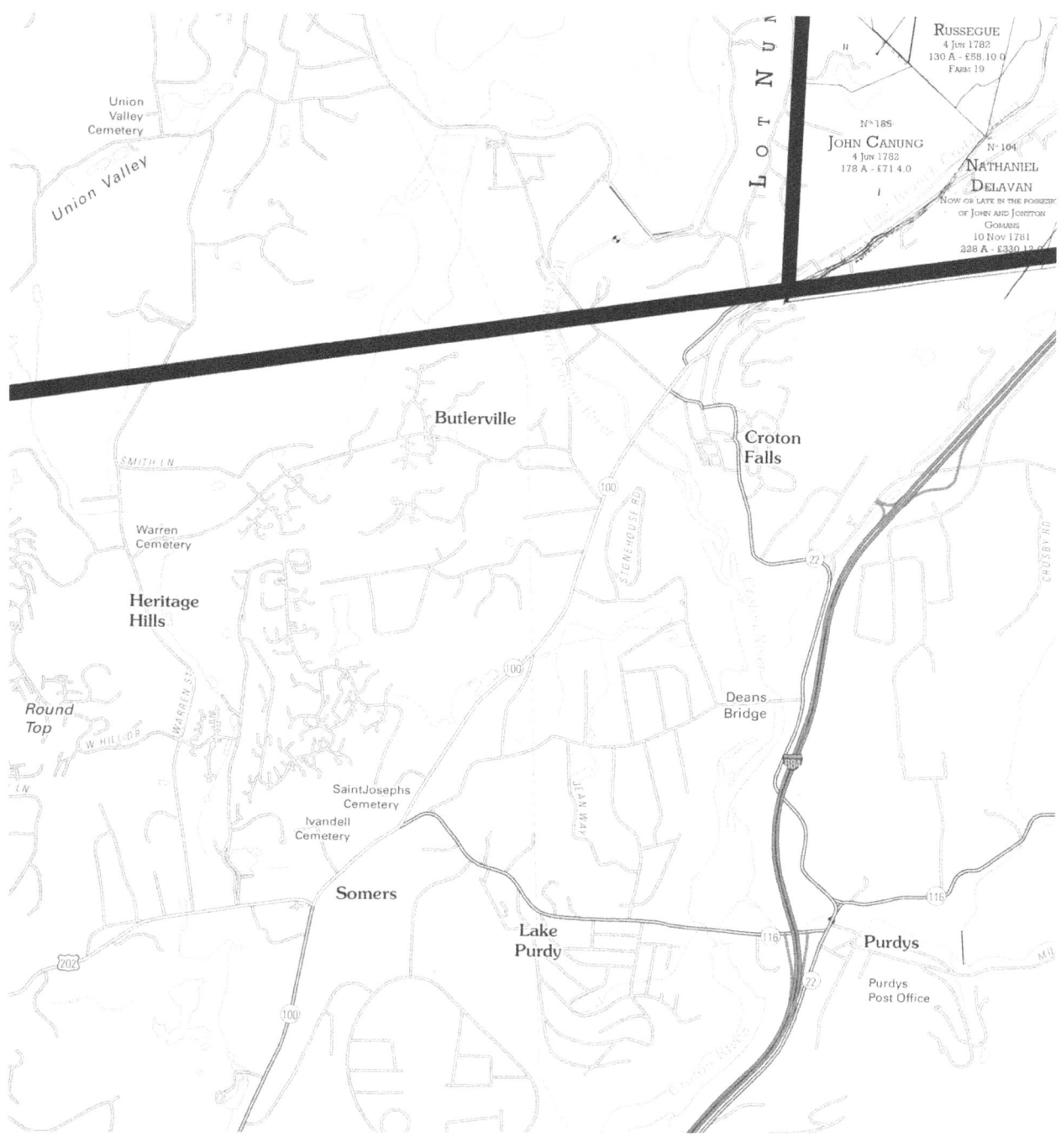

map continues on page 44

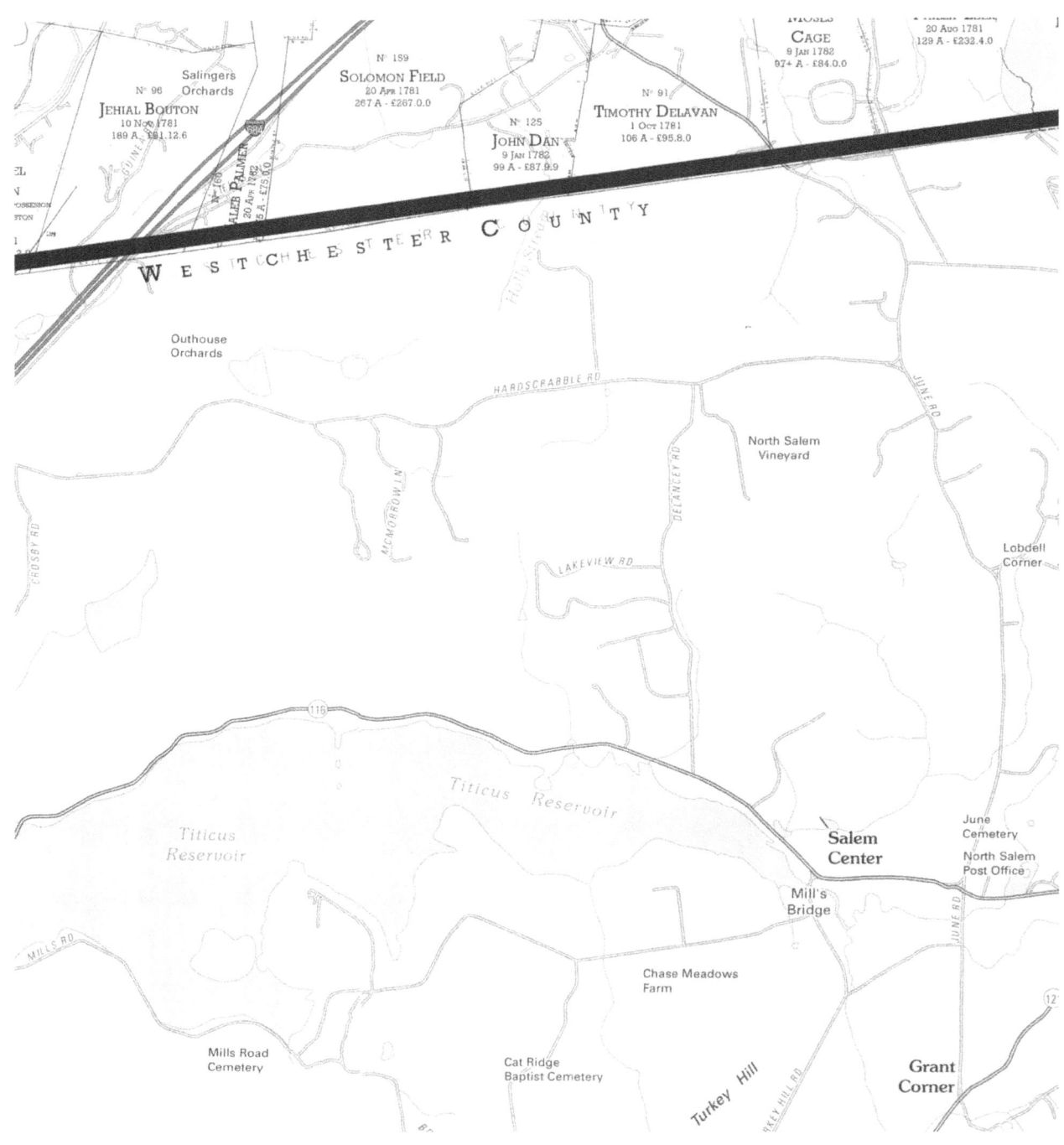

map continues on page 45

Name Index

Adams, John	12, 13, 42	Barrel, Justice	20
Adams, Thomas	13, 15, 34	Barret, Isaac	12, 13, 17, 18, 19, 20
Adriance, Cornelius	15, 23	Barret, James	17
Agar, Charles	12, 42	Barret, Justus	21
Akin, David	8	Barrett, Isaac	13, 33
Akin, Joseph	8	Barrett, Isaac	13
Akin, Josias	19	Barrett, Justis	18
Akins, David	8, 9	Barrit, Isaac	18
Akins, Jonathan	16	Barton, John	15, 17, 31
Alger, Wm B.	18, 27	Bashford, Thomas	16, 20, 48
Algers, William	9	Bayley, Peleg	12
Ambler, John	35	Bea, Isaac	12, 41
Anderson, Daniel	31	Beadsley, Andrew	8
Anderson, Nathaniel	20	Beardsley, Benajah	28
Anderson, Peter	12, 13, 14, 41	Bedeau, Isaac	14, 41
Anderson, Peter	41	Bedeau, Peter	11, 14, 41
Angevine, Wedow	9, 49	Bell, Peter	16, 18, 19, 40
Archer, Gabriel	15, 17, 40, 48	Bennet, Increase	8
Armstrong, John	14, 15, 16, 17, 40	Bennett, Increase	28
Arwas, Charles	13	Berret, Isaac	18
Arway, Charles	12, 13, 16	Berrett, Isaac	34
Atkins, David	8	Berrett, James	34
Atkins, Josiah	8	Berrit, Justice	18, 26
Austin, Isaac	13, 14, 41	Berritt, James	17
Austin, Jonathan	10, 13, 41	Berry, Jabez	9, 11, 42
Avory, John	11, 12, 13, 14, 41	Berry, John	9, 11, 12, 13, 41, 42
Ayers, Richard	33	Beya, John	14, 49
Ayres, Richard	18, 19	Beya , John	14
Badde, Isaac	11	Birch, John	11
Baddeau, Isaac	14	Birdsall, Abraham	8, 9, 19, 28
Baddeau, Peter	14	Birdsall, James	21
Bailey, Jeremiah	9	Birdsall, John	8, 9
Bailey, John, Jr.	12, 13, 25	Bloomer, Benjamin	15
Bailey, Peleg	10, 16	Bloomer, Benjamin	15, 17, 20, 30
Bailey, Peleg	16	Bloomer, Gilbert	16
Bailey, Samuel	10	Bloomer, Gilbert	15, 16, 19, 20, 30
Baker, Abraham	21, 39	Bloomer, William	9, 11
Baker, AbrM	21	Bolden, James	12
Baker, Squire	17, 19, 31	Bond, Moses	16
Ballard, Tracy	8, 9	Boomer, Benjamin	20
Ballard, William	16, 34	Boothe, John	14, 17, 19, 33
Ballard, Wilm.	20	Bouton, Jehial	10, 11, 52
Banker, Peter	11, 13, 41	Boyd, Ebenezer	10, 17, 18, 19, 20, 21, 25, 26, 33, 34, 48
Banker, Peter, Dec	14		
Barager, John	13	Boyds, Ebenezer	10, 16
Barager, Peter	13, 19, 20, 48	Brinkerhoff, John	17, 19, 31, 32
Bard, Joseph	15, 17, 18, 20, 21, 40	Brower, Hannah	13, 49
Bardsley, Benajah	12, 50	Brower, John	18

Name Index

Brower, Teunis	18	Cole, Elijah	13, 15
Browers, Hannah	12	Cole, Elijah, Jr.	13, 15
Brown, Jonathan	9, 11, 44	Cole, Elisha	16, 34, 42
Brown, Josiah	11, 43	Cole, Joseph	13, 34, 42
Bryant, Dr. Samuel	8	Cole, Solomon	34
Bryant, Thomas	13	Colegrove, William	16, 18, 19, 40
Bryon, Thomas	11	Concklin, John	17
Budd, Gilbert	21	Concklin, Mary	14, 15, 17, 18, 48
Budd, John	17, 19, 23	Concklin, Stephen	10
Bugby, Daniel	15	Cook, Jas.	12
Bugby, Ezekiel	19	Cornell, Solomon	20
Bugby/Higby, Daniel	41	Covert, Sylvenus	13, 14, 49
Bull, Daniel	11	Covey, James	8, 9, 28
Burch, Daniel	16	Covey, John	8, 9
Burch, John	8, 9, 28	Covy, James	18
Burch, John, Widow of David	8	Cowen, David	10, 11, 44
Burch, Jonathan	8, 9, 27	Crab, John	12, 42
Burch, Widow	8	Crabe, Jonathan	9
Burch, Widow of David	8, 28	Craft, John	11
Burling, Ebenezer S.	11	Crane, John	9, 13, 42
Bush, Daniel	19	Crane, Jonathan	9, 44
Cage, Moses	44	Crane, Jonathan	9, 44
Cain, John	9	Crane, Joseph, Jr.	15
Calkins, James	9, 29	Crane, Lewis, Carpenter, John. Sarah, Caleb	11
Campbell, John	21		
Canfield, Jedediah	21	Crane, Tamar	42
Canung, John	51	Crankite, Teunis	17, 33
Carie, Samuel	16	Crankright, Teunis	18
Carl, Camuel ? Samuel	17	Crawfoot, Joseph	8
Carle, Samuel	16, 17, 19, 25	Crawford, William	13, 15, 24
Carles, Isaac	18	Cromwell, Judith	16, 17, 30
Carles, Samuel	19	Cromwell, Samuel	15, 48
Carles, William	17	Cromwell, Wedow	15
Carley, Peter	8, 28	Cronk, Sibert	20, 40
Carpenter, Caleb & wife Amy	42	Cronkhite, Tunis	19
Carpenter, Epharim	10, 19	Crosby, Ben	44
Carpenter, Wedw Hannah	11, 42	Crosby, Benjamin	9, 10, 11, 43
Carrell, Samuel	17	Crosby, Enoch	9, 43, 44
Carver, Timothy	13, 14, 15, 42	Crosby, Nathan	8, 9, 36
Chadwick, Comfort	11, 14, 15, 16, 17, 18, 33, 34	Crosby, Solomon	10, 11, 15, 44
Chandler, Joseph	9, 15, 16, 18, 27, 36	Crowfoot, Joseph	27
Charlick, Henry	10, 14, 18, 19, 20, 21, 26	Cudney, Jeremiah	15, 20
Chase, Daniel	9	Cummins, Mary Ann	40
Chase, Mary	13	Curry, George	14
Chase, WedW	9, 15, 17	Curry, Wife of John Curry	41
Christian, John	18, 20, 40	Cushman, Consider	18, 26
Christian, Richard	13, 16, 18, 21	Dakin, Johnson	19
Christian, Richard, Jr.	13, 17, 40	Dan, John	9, 10, 11, 52
Christian, Richard, Senr	15, 40	Davis, John	14, 15, 18, 20 34
Clark, Abigail	9, 11, 14, 42	Deakins, Johnson	21, 26
Close, David	8, 28	Delavan, Abraham	9, 11, 44
Close, David, Rev.	8	Delavan, Daniel	16
Cock, James	9, 11, 14, 41, 42	Delavan, Nathaniel	8, 9, 10, 28, 51
Cole, Daniel	13, 34, 42	Delavan, Samuel	8, 10, 13, 28, 41
Cole, Ebenezer	12, 14, 34	Delavan, Timothy	9, 10, 11, 52

Name Index

Delavan, William	13
Denny, John	15, 18, 41, 49
Denny, Richard	15, 17, 18 31, 40
Dibble, David	15, 27
Dibbles, David	8
Dickenson, John	44
Dickerson, John	9, 10, 11, 44
Doty, Abner	10, 11, 16, 44
Drake, Capt. John	11
Drake, John	9, 14, 15, 19, 42, 48
Drake, John (son of William)	10
Drake, Joshua	16, 32
Drake, Peter	10
Drake, Samuel	10, 16, 17, 18, 20, 32, 47, 48
Drew, Isaac	17, 18, 20, 33
Dubois, Peter	15, 17 20, 22, 30
Duer, William	8, 9
Duer, William, Esq.	9, 13, 36
Dunn, James	13, 34
Dusenbury, Moses	14, 20, 48
Dusenbury, Moses, Jr.	13, 20, 40, 48
Dusenbury, William	10, 13, 14, 18, 20, 48
Dutton, William	8
Ellis, Jacob	9, 10, 12, 43
Ellis, James	12
Elsworth, John	15
Fairley, James	18, 29
Falkiner, Josiah	20
Farrington, Joseph	8, 19, 26, 34
Ferris, Reed	9, 13
Field, Anthony	10, 15, 16, 18, 19, 40
Field, John	10, 44
Field, Joseph	10
Field, Solomon	9, 11, 44, 52
Field, Stephen	9, 10, 11, 12, 44
Field, William	11, 12, 43
Folkner, Josiah	11, 13, 32
Forbes, Paul S.	16, 33
Foster, Duke	10, 12, 21, 43, 44
Fowler, Caleb	8
Frisby, Caleb	8, 16, 28, 36
Frost, David	15, 17, 18, 34
Frost, Jedediah	15, 21, 39, 41
Fulkener, Josiah	14
Fuller, Robert	9, 20, 34
Gage, Moses	10, 11, 13
Gager, Nathaniel	12, 18, 20, 40
Ganung, John	12, 13
Garnaus, John	20
Gauger, Nathaniel	12, 40
Gearnau, John	12, 16
Gee, Ezekiel	9, 16, 17, 21, 32
Gegory, Joseph	42
Gernau, John	17
Gharlick, Henry	9
Gifford, Benjamin	15
Gilchrist, William	11, 15, 27, 51
Gomans, John	10, 51
Gomans, Jonathan	51
Gomans, Jonston	18
Goodfellow, William	8, 18, 19, 26
Gove, John	9, 39, 44
Governeur, Mary M.	9
Graham, Charles	9, 11, 12, 41
Graham, Charles F.	9
Grant, James	14, 16
Gray, John	12
Green, Benjamin	9
Green, Nathan	9, 10, 11, 15, 44
Gregory, Ezra	9, 10, 43
Gregory, Joseph	9, 11, 12, 14, 15, 40
Gregory, Josiah	15
Griffen, Jacob	10, 13, 24
Grove, John	12
Grun, Nathan	18
Haight, Amy	15, 18, 19
Haight, Capt. John	11
Haight, Captain	13
Haight, Gilbert	14, 41
Haight, John	11, 12, 23
Haight, Samuel	12, 14
Haigt, Gilbert	12, 14
Haigt, Gilbert	12
Haigt, Samuel	8
Hains, Asa	10
Hains, John	10
Hains, Mary	43
Hains, Mary	9
Hains, Samuel	10, 40
Hains, Widown Mary	9
Hanion, David	8, 17, 19, 24, 31
Hans, Asa	18
Harrington, Joseph	11, 26
Haskin, Joseph	9, 12, 44
Hatch, Timothy	9, 15
Haviland, Isaac	18
Hawkins, Isabell	18, 16
Hawkins, Samuel	8, 16 18, 19, 20, 26, 34
Haynes, Asa	35
Hays, James	9, 18, 36
Headon, William	18
Headon, William	14, 41
Heady, William	17, 18, 20
Healey, Ebenezer	17
Healey, Eleazer	19, 31
Healey, John	8, 19
Hecock, David	8, 9, 13, 28
Heroy, Charles	13, 18, 49
Hichcock, William	15

Name Index

Higby, Daniel	14, 15, 17
Higby, William	14, 15, 41, 50
Hill, Capt.	8, 12
Hill, Capt. William	11
Hill, David	8, 9, 19, 21, 28
Hill, Thomas	12, 15, 17, 18, 40
Hill, Wedow	12, 13, 42
Hill, William	11, 41
Hitchcock, William	11, 13, 14, 15, 16, 41, 42
Hitcock, William	14
Hopkins, Isaiah	14, 16, 20, 34
Hopkins, Jesse	12
Hopkins, Solomon	13, 14, 16, 17, 18, 19, 20, 33, 34, 50
Hopkis, Solomon	17
Horton, John	13, 16, 18, 40, 49
Horton, Joseph	10
Horton, Joshua	16, 18, 19, 20, 41
Horton, Thomas	12, 17, 19, 25
Hoskin, Joseph	41
How, John	9, 11
Howes, Moody	9, 11, 16, 44
Howkins, Samuel	12
Hoyat, Abraham	11, 12
Hoyat, John	12, 13, 20, 49
Huestis, Charity	20
Huestis, Wedow Charity	14
Hughson, Jeremiah	13, 15, 16, 50
Hughson, Robert	13, 20, 42
Hunt, Daniel	16, 33
Hunt, Elijah	14, 19, 33
Hunt, Isaac	8
Hunt, Jesse	44
Hunt, Jesse	18
Hunt, Samuel	15, 17, 18, 20, 41
Hunt, Thomas	16, 17
Husted, Charity	10
Husted, Joseph	15, 17
Husted, Wedow	12, 15, 17
Hustin, Robert	12, 20
Hustis, Charity	15
Hustis, Joseph	15, 31
Hustis, Joseph	15
Hustis, Wedow Charity	15, 31, 50
Hyatt, Abraham	9, 17
Hyatt, Col. John	13, 18
Hyatt, John	13, 14, 16, 17, 18, 20, 21, 25, 32, 33
Hyatt, John & Co.	13, 16, 17, 18
Hyatt, Joshua	13, 14, 32
Hyatt, Nathaniel	13, 14, 17, 32
Ingorsel,	16
Jacocks, James	16, 17, 32, 40
Jacox, David P.	9
James, John	19
James, Samuel	11
Jean, John	8, 11, 44
Johnson, Samuel	9
Jones, Epharim	9, 18, 36
Jones, Samuel	17, 18, 24, 33
Ketchem, "Lot"	12
Kich, Thomas	8, 42
Kidd, Alexander	10, 11, 28
Kidd, Esq.	36
Kidd, Joseph	8, 19
Kiers, Henry	12, 19, 32
King, Herman	11, 44, 49
Kirkham, Thomas	13, 49
Kirkham, Zebedee	13, 49
Kirkum, Thomas	16
Kirkum, Zebulon	16
Knap, Benjamin	13, 16, 19
Knap, Daniel	13, 14, 49
Knap, Hannah	13, 14, 25
Knap, Israel	14, 16, 17, 19
Knap, Moses	13, 14, 19, 41
Knapp, Benjamin	25, 49
Knapp, Hannah	17
Knapp, Israel	12, 23
Knaps, Hannah	11
Knaps, Moses	12, 16
Kniffin, Jacob	17, 19, 50
Krankright, Sibert	16
Krankright, Teunis	19
Kronkhight, Sibert	17
Kronkrite, Lawrence	9
Laclare, John	13
Lane, George	17, 20
Lane, George	13, 14, 17, 32, 49
Lane, Hyatt	12, 40
Lane, Nathan	13, 14, 17, 49
Langdon, James	12, 17, 24
Le Clare, John	10, 12, 42
Leak, Phillip	11, 12
LeClere, John	12, 19
Lee, Caleb	9, 26
Leek, Phillip	10, 44
Lewis, Ichabod	42
Lewis, Sarah, wife of Henry	17
Lewis, Thomas	16, 17, 19
Light, Henry	16, 18, 20
Likely, John	8, 19, 21, 40
Lindsey, David	11
Lockwood, Ebenezer	11, 12, 13, 14, 15, 34, 42
Lockwood, Gilbert	9, 16, 17, 19, 44, 48
Lockwood, Timothy	16, 44
Longwell, David	19
Lott, Phillip	49
Lounsbery, Isaac	10, 12

Name Index

Loveless, William	9, 10, 12, 44	Newman, William	14
Lowrie, Thomas	8, 44	Nickerson, Edward	10, 18, 19, 20, 21, 26
Luddington, Comfort	8, 9, 11, 28	Nickerson, Hannah	10, 43
Luddington, Henry	8	Nickerson, Wedow	41
Luddington, Henry	28	Nielson, Mahar	10
Ludington, Comfort	15	Nott, Nathaniel	10, 12, 44, 49
Mabee, Abraham	11, 42	O'Brian, John	15
Mabee, Peter	16, 42	O'Bryant, Thomas	13
Mabey, John	13	O'Byan, Catherine	13, 33
Mahar, Nelson	14, 28	Oakely, Gilbert	28
Markay, John	16	Oakley, Elijah	8, 18
Marsh, Capt. Dubois	15	Oakley, Gilbert	12, 18, 20
Marvin, Ichabad	10, 15, 44	Oakley, John	12, 13, 18, 42
Matine, John	18	Oakley, Mary	12
Maybee, Abraham	11, 18	Oakley, Robert	12, 18, 33
Maybee, Peter	12, 15	Oakley, Wedow	10
McCabe, Matthew	16, 40, 41	Oakley, William	17
McClean, John	13	Obrian, Catherine	17
McDonald, John	13, 15, 16, 41	Obrian, John	18
McKabe, Mathew	11, 16	Odle, Amos	10, 17, 18
McLean, John	12, 13, 21	Odle, Benjamin	10, 20, 48
McLean, Johnson	9	Odle, Isaac	10, 17, 40
Mead, Edmond	9, 10, 11, 44	Odle, Jonathan	16, 31
Mead, Jeremiah	10, 20, 44	Odle, Oliver	16, 17, 19, 20, 41
Mead, Moses	9, 16, 26	Ogden, Joseph	12, 18, 19
Mead , Jeremiah	21	Owen, Jesse	10, 12, 48
Meed, Edmond	16	Owen, Jonathan	14, 15, 16, 17
Meek, John	20, 21	Owens, Jesse	16
Meeks, John	8	Owens, Jonathan	16, 19, 40, 46, 48
Melgram, Alexander	8	Owens, Joshua	10
Menzies, Thomas	11	Paddock, David	10, 10
Merrit, John	14, 41	Paddock, David, Jr.	9, 10, 45
Merritt, John	34	Paddock, Seth	9, 44
Merritt, Joseph	15	Paddock, Silas	9, 10, 44
Miller, Jonathan	8, 15, 16, 18, 40	Paddock, Zachariah	10, 44
Mills, Samuel	8, 11, 28	Paine, Joseph	10, 48
Mills, William Smith's	8	Palmer, Caleb	9, 11, 52
Mitchell, Thomas	8, 17	Palmer, William	10, 36
Monger, Lemuel	14, 18, 19, 33	Patterson, Esq.	8
Montross, Peter	8	Patterson, Mathew	8, 10, 11, 18, 28, 36
Mooney, Robert	9, 10, 14, 28	Patterson, Mathew, Esq.	18, 28
Morris, Mary	8	Pearce, Isaac	10, 36, 43
Morris, Robert	9, 28, 34	Pell, Philip	8, 9
Morris, Roger & Wife	19, 41	Pell, Phillip, Esq.	8
Mory , David	10	Pell, Samuel	8
Moss, Joseph	18, 26	Pell, Samuel T.	21, 36
Moss, Mary	19	Pelton, Benjamin	10, 21, 24
Munger, Lemuel	14	Pelton, Daniel	10, 12, 24
Myrick, Joshua	20, 32, 41	Pelton, Philip	10, 12, 14, 16, 17, 18, 19, 32, 41
Nealy, Rebecka	19, 20		
Nelson, Justus	12, 20	Penier, Isaac	18
Nelson, Mahar	8	Penier, Isaac	12, 17, 28, 33, 49
Newberry, John	8, 9, 25, 28	Perces, Isaac	13
Newcomb, Zacheus	15, 19	Perry, James	8, 13, 40
Newman, Nathaniel	13	Phillips, Ebenezer	32, 43

Name Index

Phillips, Frederick, et. al.	8
Phillips, Jacob	8, 9
Phillips, James	8, 28
Phillips, Phillip	9, 10, 40
Phillipse, Frederick	9, 33, 39
Pierce, Isaac	44
Pinckney, Frederick	10, 11, 19, 36, 44
Pinckney, Isreal	10
Pine, Jonathan	10, 19, 32
Pinkney, Frederick	11
Pinkney, Isreal	10, 12
Platt, John	10, 12, 55
Platt, Zephaniah	13, 20, 25
Platts, John	10, 11, 17
Platts, Zephaniah & Co.	16, 18, 19
Porter, David	14, 19, 21, 26
Post, Abraham	8, 14, 18, 41
Post, Anthony	9, 10, 11, 17, 28
Post, Henry	8, 19, 20, 40
Post, John	17, 20, 41
Post & Odle, Henry & Isaac	39
Potts, George H.	18
Price, Ebenezer	19
Price, James	18
Price, Mary	26, 28
Price,	19
Prindle, Lattice	8, 13
Purdy, Wedow	19, 24
Randle, Joseph	12, 17, 19, 26
Read, Isaac	14, 16
Read, Jacob	43, 48
Ressegue, Isaac	20
Rhodes, Isaac	14, 15, 19, 20, 34, 41
Rhodes, James	41
Rhodes, John	10
Rice, Edward	9, 10, 11, 45
Richards, Ezra	9, 10, 11, 44
Richards, Moses	10, 15, 44
Rickey, Peter	11, 15, 21, 47
Roads, Isaac	12, 13, 17, 19, 41
Roads, Jacob	18
Roads, John	17, 18
Roads, Mary	12, 17
Roads, Shanadore	10, 12
Roberts, Peter	8, 12
Robinson, Beverly	9
Robinson, John	12
Rodes, John	14
Rondle, Joseph	10
Rosekrans, James	17, 28
Rubbleyee, Andrew	12
Russegue, Isaac	12, 18
Russel, John	13, 16, 33
Russel, Robert	13, 14, 15, 19 34
Russel, Thomas	14, 15, 19, 41
Russell, John	12
Russell, Robert	13, 20
Ryall, John	9, 19, 25
Ryall, Peter	9, 19, 25
Sacket, James	11, 44
Sacket, James	44
Sands, Comfort	9, 29, 33, 36
Saterly, Richard	8, 13, 18, 21
Scott, Peter	10
Scribner, Nathaniel	14
Secor, Isaac	14, 41
Secor, John	8, 14, 41
Shaw, Daniel	8, 9, 18, 28
Shaw, Robert	16, 18, 19, 20, 33
Shaw, William	21, 33
Sheldon, Nathan	19
Sherwood, James	14, 48
Sherwood, Joseph	18
Simkins, John	18, 33
Simkins, Robert	12
Slutt, Michael	11, 12, 13, 19, 42
Smalley, James	11, 18
Smalley, John	34
Smith, Col. William	12, 41
Smith, David	12, 16
Smith, Davis	12
Smith, Elijah	12, 13, 19, 39
Smith, James C.	11
Smith, John	12, 13, 18, 41
Smith, Joseph	13, 15, 18, 49
Smith, Maurice	20, 26
Smith, Mauris	14
Smith, Morris	10, 15, 19, 20
Smith, Mourice	19, 31
Smith, Seth	13
Smith, Solomon	13, 14, 16, 41
Smith, Thomas	8, 19, 48
Smith, William	9, 12, 17, 41, 42
Smith & Read, Thomas & Jacob	32
Snouck, John	20
Snouck, Mathew	17, 20
Sparling, Paul	17, 18, 20, 31
Sprage, Jeremiah	16, 19
Sprague, Jeremiah	17, 26, 34
Springer, Isaac	9, 19, 20, 32
St. John, Abraham	28, 36
Stebbens, Nehemiah	15
Steenbach, Philip	15, 20, 40
Steenback, Phillip	17
Steenbauck, Philip	17
Steneback, Philip	9
Stephens, Nathaniel	8
Stibbens, Nehemiah	12
Stokom, Jonathan	11, 12, 42

Name Index

Surrine, Charles	11, 12, 42
Surrione, James	11
Surroin, Charles	12
Surroin, James	9, 49
Surroine, James	19
Swarthwout, Jacobus	15, 19, 21
Swift, Josiah	16
Sylvenus, Covert	19
Taylor, Daniel	12, 18, 25, 26
Taylor, Isaac	13, 15, 33
Taylor, Thomas	20
Ter Boss, Daniel	20, 22, 30
Ter Bush, Daniel	18
Terry, Peter	15
Tidd (kidd?), Joseph	15
Tompkin, Nathaniel	15
Tompkins, Cornelius	15, 16, 18, 40
Tompkins, Jonathan G.	20
Tompkins, Joshua	18, 20, 41
Tompkins, Josiah	18
Tompkins, Nathan	18
Tompkins, Nathaniel	16, 20, 40
Tompkins, Reuben	8, 18, 20, 36, 41
Towner, Samuel	9, 20
Townsend, Benjamin	34
Townsend, Charles	9, 10, 20, 34
Townsend, Christopher	10, 11, 15, 16, 44
Townsend, Daniel	9
Townsend, Elihu	9
Townsend, Isaac	16
Townsend, James	11, 12, 18, 19, 20, 34
Townsend, Job	10, 49
Townsend, John	10, 11, 16, 20, 26, 44
Townsend, Levi	18, 20, 34
Townsend, Levy	9, 15, 20
Townsend, Robert	9
Townsend, Robert, Dec	10
Townsend, Uriah	11
Townsend, Uriah	15
Travis, Titus	12, 18, 41
Trobridge, Billy	28, 50
Trowbridge, Billy	8, 15
Turner, Nathan	36
Utter, Amos	8, 9
Utters, John	19, 30
Van Ambler, John	20
Van Amburgh, John	21
Van Scoy, Abel	26
Van Scoy, Timothy	17, 19
Van Tassel, Easter	21, 40
Van Tassel, Wedw Hester	9, 16
Van Wert, Isaac	16
Vanamber, John	13
Vanscoy, Abel	13, 14, 17, 18, 19, 20, 26, 34
Vanscoy, Jacob	14, 15, 16, 34
Vansqoit, Jacob	44
Vantassel, WidW. Hester	8
Vermillion, John	11
Vermillion, John, Late	10
Vorkaneer, Josiah	9
Wainer, Jesse	8
Wall, Stone	9
Wallace, Uriah	9, 10, 12, 16, 28, 44
Ward, Isreal	8
Ward, Stephen, Esq.	15, 18
Warden, Nathaniel	9
Waring, Epharim	10
Waring, Thaddeus	8, 10, 11, 43
Warner, Jesse	8, 10, 28
Warrin, Epharim	13
Watt, Robert	8
Weed, Jehial	8, 11, 15
Weeks, Gilbert	9, 14, 15, 17, 20, 23
Weisenfell, Charles F.	10
White, William	9, 18, 19, 40, 50
Whitney, Jeremiah	13, 21
Wichell, Timothy	8
Wicksom, Peleg	28
Wilcox, Roswell	12, 16
Willet, Gilbert	17
Williams, Francis	8, 14, 17, 33
Williams, Richard	8
Willis, Jedediah	16, 35, 48
Willsie, Daniel	10, 14, 16
Wiltsey, Daniel	16, 17, 19
Wiltsey, Henry	19
Wiltsey, Martin	10, 14, 16, 19, 20, 30
Winter, Moses	12, 18, 20, 26, 41
Wisenfells, Charles F.	42
Wixsom, Peleg	8, 9, 11, 12
Wixsom, Shubal	11, 12
Wolf, Sarah	10, 17
Wood, Mary	10
Wood, Nehemiah	9, 10, 11, 12, 44
Wood, Robert	8
Wright, Daniel	9
Wright, Dennis	11, 23
Wright, Wiilliam	8, 11, 17, 20, 28
Wyllis, Jedediah	14, 18
Wynn, John	13, 32
Wynn, Joseph	12
Yeoman, Anthony	9
Yeoman, Samuel	13, 14, 20
Yeoman, William	25
Yeomans, John	11, 20
Yeomans, William	40, 41

Place Index

Acker Kill	12
Adriance	17
Allen Corners	34
An Old Corner	17
Anthonys Nose	46
Anthonys Nose Beacon	46
Arden Point	38
Bailey Cemetery	34
Bald Hill	23
Baldwin Place	49
Ballard Ground Cemetery	27
Ballard Lake	26
Banger Pond	49
Bare Hill	27
Bare Rock Mountain	38
Barnum Corners	37
Barrett Pond	31, 34
Beacon	22
Beacon Hills	23
Beacon Reservoir	22, 23
Beacon-Newburgh Ferry	22
Bear Mountain Bridge	46
Beardslee	9
Beaver Brook	12
Beaver Dam Brook	13
Benjamin	8
Berkshire Terrace	26
Berry	14
Bever Creek	21
Beverdam Brook	21
Beverly Dock	46
Beverly Hills Cemetery	48
Birch Hill	29
Black Pond	25
Black Pond Brook	25
Bog Brook Reservoir	44
Bog Meadow	8, 9, 13
Boggs Pond	45
Boyd	17
Boyd Corners Reservoir	34
Break Neck Hill	15
Breakneck Point	30
Breakneck Ridge	30
Brewster	44
Brewster Heights	44
Brewster Hill	36
Brewster Pond	36
Brimston Mountain	29
Broccy Creek Reservoir	46
Brockway	22
Brook & Highway Brook	14
Browns Mountain	37
Browns Pond	27
Bryant Pond	41
Bull Hill	30
Burlin	9
Burling	12
Butlerville	51
Buttermilk Falls	16, 19, 38
Cable Corn	53
California Hill	33
Camp Herrich	28, 26
Camp Hines	34
Camp Merrywood	28
Camp Wiccopee	32
Canada Hill	46
Candlewood Hill	40
Canopus Creek	32, 40, 47
Canopus Hill	39
Canopus Island	42
Canopus Lake	32, 40
Canopus River	15
Canopus Road	15
Carmel	35
Carmel Hills	43
Castle Rock	38, 39
Cat Hill	39
Cat Pond	39
Cat Ridge Bapt Cemetery	52
Cat Rock	47
Catfish Pond	39
Catskill Aquaduct	30, 39
Cedar Pond	12
Cedar Pond Brook	9, 12
Chadwick	17
Chase Meadows Farm	52
Chicory Meadow Farm	46, 47
China Pond	34
Christian Corners	40
Clear Lake	32
Clear Pool	34
Clove Creek	17, 31, 32
Coals Pond	17
Cold Spring	38
Cold Spring Cemetery	30
Coles Pond	16
Con Hook	46
Conger Hill	29

Place Index

Connecticut Line	15	Fairview Cemetery	22
Constitution Island	20, 38	Farm 1	13, 17
Continental Village	47	Farm 10	13, 14
Corlandt Lake	47	Farm 11	10, 11, 13, 15
Corner of Brook & Highway	14	Farm 12	8, 11, 13, 14
Corner Pond	37	Farm 13	11, 13, 14, 15
Corners	48	Farm 14	8, 10, 11, 15
Cornwall Hill	28	Farm 15	11, 16
Courtland Manor Line	12, 13, 14, 15, 16, 19	Farm 16	9, 10 11, 12, 14
		Farm 17	11, 12, 14, 15, 16
Crafts	43	Farm 18	8, 10, 14, 16
Cranberry Mountain	29	Farm 19	12
Cranberry Pond	11, 42	Farm 2	13, 14
Crane Cemetery	42	Farm 20	8, 14, 16, 18
Crofts Corners	40	Farm 21	8, 12
Croton Bridge	8	Farm 22	10, 12
Croton River	8, 9, 10, 11, 12, 13, 15, 16, 18, 19	Farm 23	8, 10, 14
		Farm 24	18, 19, 20
Crows nest	38	Farm 25	8, 13, 14, 15
Crows nest brook	38	Farm 26	8, 9, 11, 13, 14
Crystal Lake	46	Farm 27	8, 9, 11, 14, 15, 19
Dale Pond	38	Farm 28	9, 11, 14, 15, 18
Dam Mill	11	Farm 29	8, 11, 14, 18
Deans Bridge	51	Farm 29	8
Deans Corner	44	Farm 3	13, 14, 15, 17
Deforest Corners	37	Farm 30	11, 14, 18
Denning Hill	39	Farm 31	8, 9, 14
Denning Point	22	Farm 32	8, 20
Dennytown	32	Farm 32	20
Denton Lake	27	Farm 33	14, 15
Dickenson	10	Farm 34	11, 20
Dickenson & Bull Mill	9	Farm 35	16
Dickerson	10	Farm 36	11, 16
Dixon Lake	42	Farm 37	11, 15, 16
Dolittle	17	Farm 38	11, 14
Drewscliff Cemetery	44	Farm 39	8
Drewville Heights	44	Farm 4	11, 13, 17
Duck Island	38	Farm 40	8, 16
Duck Pond	39	Farm 41	9, 14, 15
Dutch South Line	9, 10	Farm 42	16
Dutchess Junction	30	Farm 43	8, 9, 11, 14
Dwelling house	19	Farm 44	14
Dykemans	36	Farm 46	8, 10, 20
East Branch Croton River	28, 37, 44, 51	Farm 47	10, 20
East Branch Reservoir	44, 45	Farm 48	8
East Corner of Lott 2	14	Farm 49	8, 12, 14, 15
East Gable	46	Farm 5	8, 12, 13, 14, 17
East Line	11	Farm 50	1, 14
East Line	12	Farm 51	11, 12, 14
East Mountain	31	Farm 52	8, 11, 14, 15
East of Lott 4 Line	14	Farm 53	11
East of Water Lotts Line	17	Farm 55	8, 11
Ellis Cemetery	43	Farm 56	8
Episcopal Church	10	Farm 57	11
Fahnestock Ski Slope	33	Farm 58	11

Place Index

Farm 59	11	Grove	9, 10
Farm 6	11, 13, 14, 15	Groveville	22
Farm 60	11, 14	Haines Corners	36
Farm 61	12, 13	Haines Pond	45
Farm 62	11, 13	Harmony Park	28
Farm 63	11, 12, 13, 14	Haviland Hollow	29
Farm 64	15	Haviland Hollow Brook	29
Farm 7	9, 10, 12, 14, 15	Haycock	18
Farm 70	13, 14	Heady Pond	11, 12, 14
Farm 71	12	Hemlock Hollow	21
Farm 72	13	Heritage Hills	51
Farm 8	12, 13, 14, 15	Hiden Meadow Farms	44
Farm 9	11, 14, 15	High Cliff	12
Farm 96	11	Highland Falls	38
Farm Lot 1	15	Highland Patent	9
Farm Lot 2	15	Hill Water River	14
Farm Mill	9, 12	Hitchcock Hill	42
Farrell Hill	36	Holmes	27
Farringtons Pond	45	Horse Pound Brook	35
Feeds Heady Brook	14	Horton Estates	50
Field Corners	35	Hortontown	25
Fishkill Farms	24	Hosner Mountain	25
Fishkill Highway	13	Hudson River	15, 16, 17, 19
Forsonville	39	Hustin's Pond	9, 11, 16, 42
Fort Defiance Hill	39	Hustins Island	11
Fort Hill	39, 47	Ice Pond	36
Fort Montgomery	46	Indian Brook	38, 39
Foshay Corners	25, 33	Indian Lake	39
Foundry Brook	31	Isaac Springer	32
Four Mile Lot	8, 10	Ivandell Cemetery	51
Fredericksburgh & Phillips Line	16, 17, 18, 19, 20	Jacox Pond	31
Fredericksburgh Line	21	Jefferson Village	49
Gallows Hill	47	John Pond	25
Gant Corner	52	Johnson	8
Garrison	38	Jonathan Akins Road	16
Garrison Four Courners	38	Jones Hill	48
Garrison Pond	46	Jones Pond	44
Gee Point	38	Jordan Pond	32
Gerow Millpond	29	June Cemetery	52
Gilbert Corners	40	Kannopus Road	15
Gilead Cemetry	43	Kelly Cemetery	35
Glenclyffe	38	Kent Cliffs	34
Glencoma Lake	50	Kent Cliffs Bapt Burying Grounds	33
Glenham	23	Kent Corners	35
Gordons Brook	30	Kent Hills	27
Gore Line	18, 19	Kiah Hill	40
Granite Mountain	40	Kich Pond	12
Graymoor	47	Kings Dock	46
Graymoor Society of the Atonement Cemetery	47	Kirk Lake / Pond	42
		Kirk Pond	12
Great Pond	12, 14, 42	Knapp's Pond	49
Grist Mill	10, 19	Knaps Pond	14
Groton Falls	51	Knaps pond Brook	15
Groton Falls Resuervoir	43	Lain's Brook	18, 19
Groton River	51	Lake Alice	47

Place Index

Lake Carmel	35	Marys Meadow	46
Lake Casse	42	Matine	9
Lake Celeste	47	Maynard Corners	35
Lake Charles	37	McKeel Corners	31
Lake Dutchess	27	McLaughlin Acres	42
Lake Gilead	43	McLean	14
Lake Gleneida	35, 43	Mead	10, 12, 20
Lake Lincolndale	50	Mead Cemetery	26
Lake Mahopac	42	Meadow	19
Lake Mahopac Ridge	42	Meeting House	10
Lake Mohegan	48	Melzingah Reservoir	30
Lake Nimaam	34	Mendel Pond	28
Lake Ossi	41	Michael Brook	35, 43
Lake Peekskill	47	Middle Branch Reservoir	43
Lake Purdy	51	Mill Brook	8
Lake Shenorock	50	Mill Lot # 8	9
Lake Tibet	33	Mill Pond	12
Lake Tibet	44	Mill River	9, 10, 21
Lake Valhalla	31	Mill's Bridge	52
Lambs Hill	23	Miller Hill	27
Lanes Brook	14, 15, 17, 19, 20	Mills Road Cemetery	52
Large Pond	13	Milltown	45
Large Rock	12	Milltown Cemetery	45
Laths Pond	39	Minthorn Pond	13, 34
Lawson Cemetery	50	Mohegan Lake	48
Lincolndale	50	Moneyhole Mountain	39
Line Oblong	10	Moose Hill	33
Little Buck Mountain Pond	26	Mopas Brook	53
Little Pond	17, 37	Moras	12
Livingston Island	46	Moras	12
Lobdel Corner	52	Morris & Philips Line	16, 19, 20
Loch Lyall	39	Morris & Philips Water lotts Line	20
Lockwood Pond	34	Morris Line	12
Long Lott	21	Morris Lott 5 & Philips Lott 6 Line	21
Long Pond	13, 14, 16, 17, 42	Mount Pisgah	43
Loretta Lake	48	Mountain Brook	29
Lost Lake	37	Mountain East of Canopus Hollow	18
Lott 1	14, 18, 19	Mountain Wood Lott	20
Lott 2	13, 14, 18	Mud Lake	32
Lott 2	9	Mud Pond	32, 42
Lott 3	13, 19	Muddy Brook	8, 21, 28
Lott 6	12	Muddy Creek	18
Ludingtonville	27	Muscoot River	49
Ludingtonville Bapt Ch Cemetery	27	Mystery Point	46
Mabey	9	Nelson Corners	39
Magazine Point	38	Nelsonvill Cemetery	30
Mahopac	42	Newburgh-Beacon Bridge	22
Mahopac Airpoint	41	Nickerson	11
Mahopac Falls	41	Noney-ledge Hill	26
Mahopac Falls Bapt Churchyard	41	North Beacon Mountain	22
Mahopac Point	42	North Dock	38
Main Road	9, 18	North East Corner	18
Manitou	46	North Highland Cemetery	31
Mantoga	46	North Line	11
Maple Avenue Cemetery	28	North Line of Morris Lot Line	10

Place Index

North Salem	53	Putnam Valley	48
North Salem Post Office	52	Quaker Church Cemetery	53
North Salem Vineyard	52	Raymond Hill Cemetery	35
Northwest of whole tract Line	17	Reeves Pond	39
Northwest of whole tract Line	17	Richardsville	33
Oakley	18	Ridgefield Golf Course	53
Oblong	8, 9, 10	Roaring Brook	33
Oblong Line	15, 16	Roaring Brook Lake	33
Oblong Monument	10	Robinson's Long Lott & Morris's Water Lott Line	20
Oceola Lake	49		
Odle	16	Robinson's Water Lot	16
Ogden	19	Rockey Ridge	8
Old Bapt Burying Ground	28	Rombout & Philips Line	13, 15
Old East West Line	20	Rombout Line	16
Osawana Corners	40	Rooring Brook	18
Osawana Lake	40	Round Hill	31
Oscawana Brook	48	Round Mountain	24, 45
Outhous Orchards	52	Round Top	50
Paddock	9	Rumbout Line	19, 20
Palmer Lake	35	Rumbout & Philips Line	19
parsonage	21	Rumbout Line	17
Patterson	28	Sacred Heart Cemetery	38
Patterson Bapt Ch Cemetery	28	Salem Center	52
Peach Lake	44, 45	Salinger Orchards	44, 52
Peach Lake Cemetery	53	Salmons Daily Brook	37
Pecksville	27	Sanfords Pond	45
Peeks Kill	12, 14, 16	Saw Mill	8
Peekskill Highway	13	Scofield Hill	30
Peekskill Hollow Creek	40	Sears Corners	37
Peekskill Road	12, 13	Secor Brook	41
Pelton Pond	32	Secor Corners	42
Petre Island	42	Secor Lake	41
Pettit Meadow	12	Secor Pond	41
Pettit Meadow	12	Senior Hill	42
Philip Philips Line	16	Seven Hills Lake	26
Philips & Fredrickburg Line	16	Shanadore Road	13, 16, 18, 19
Philips & Morris Line	15	Sharp Reservation	24
Philips Brook	39	Shenandoah	25
Philips Line	11	Shenandoah Mountain	25
Phillips	10	Shenorock	50
Phillips & Morris Line	16	Shrub Oak	48
Phillips & Morris Line	18	Shrub Oak Brook	48, 49
Phillips Precinct Line	19	Shrub Post Office	48
Pine Island	28	Small Brook	8, 11, 12, 14, 20
Pine Pond	16, 34	Snake Hill	37
Plum Brook	50	Sodom	44
Pollepel Island	30	South Beacon Mountain	22
Pond Mill	13	South Dock	38
Popolopen Bridge	46	South Highland	39
Post Road	10, 11, 15, 17, 20	South Mountain Pass	46
Post Road Brook	15	Springer's Grist Mill	19
Presbyterian Cemetery	41	Spruce Hill	40
Prospect Hill	40	Spy Pond	47
Purdys	51	Squirrel Hollow Brook	30
Putnam Lake	37	St. Francis Camp	39

Place Index

St. Joachims Cemetery	22
St. Johns	10
St. Josephs Cemeter	51
St. Lukes Cemetery	22
Starr Ridge	44
Steinbeck Corners	36
Stephens Brook	28
Stibbens	11
Still Water Brook	13
Still Water River	11, 12, 13, 14
Stillwater	49
Stillwater Pond	32
Storm King	30
Stump Pond	27
Stump Pond Stream	27
Sugarloaf Hill	46
Sunken Bog Meadow	8
Sunnybrook	40
Target Point	38
Taylor	19
Teakettle Sprout Lake	50
The Colony	8
The Gore	11
The Hill	11
The Long Pond	11, 19
The Shingle Tree	19
The Small Pond	13
The Top Hill	17
Tilly Foster	43
Tinker Hill	40
Titicus Mountain	53
Titicus Reservoir	52
Titicus River	53
Tompkins Corners	41
Tompkins Corners Cemetery	41
Tonetta Brook	44
Top Mountain	13
Towners	36
Townsend	9, 10
Trout Creek	24
Trowbridge	9
Turkey Hill	34, 52
Two Roads meet	14
Union Cemetery	26, 46
Union Valley	51
Union Valley Cemetery	51
Upper Cranberry Pond	47
Upper Patent	9
Valley Point	38
Van Wyck Homstead	23
Wades Brook	30
Waring	10
Warren Cemetery	51
Water Lott of Robinson Line	21
Watermelon Hill	42, 50
West Branch Croton River	51
West Branch Canopus Creek	40
West Branch Croton River	43
West Branch Croton River	16
West Branch Groton River	34
West Branch Reservoir	42
West Patterson	28
West Point Road	16
Westchester & Dutchess Line	16, 17, 21
Westchester Line	10, 11, 12, 15, 18
Westminster Camp	27
Westminster Lake	27
White Pond	18, 21, 26
White Rock	46
Wiccopee Brook	32
Wiccopee Creek	32
Wiccopee Pass	32
Wiccopee Reservoir	40
Wickepy Road	13
William Smith's Mills	8
Winter	19
Wixon Pond	42
Wonder Lake	27
Wycopee Road	18, 20
Yale Corners	27

www.ingramcontent.com/pod-product-compliance
Lightning Source LLC
LaVergne, TN
LVHW041400060426
835510LV00016B/1913